The Essentials of Effective Written Communication for Young Researchers and Tertiary Students

Laura Cheng Sue Sen, B.Comm, (Dist)
Communications & Public Relations,
Monash University, Dip. Industrial Chemistry.

PARTRIDGE

Copyright © 2022 by Laura Cheng Sue Sen.

ISBN:	Hardcover	978-1-5437-6995-1
	Softcover	978-1-5437-6996-8
	eBook	978-1-5437-6994-4

All rights reserved. No part of this book may be used or reproduced by any means, graphic, electronic, or mechanical, including photocopying, recording, taping or by any information storage retrieval system without the written permission of the author except in the case of brief quotations embodied in critical articles and reviews.

Because of the dynamic nature of the Internet, any web addresses or links contained in this book may have changed since publication and may no longer be valid. The views expressed in this work are solely those of the author and do not necessarily reflect the views of the publisher, and the publisher hereby disclaims any responsibility for them.

Print information available on the last page.

To order additional copies of this book, contact
Toll Free +65 3165 7531 (Singapore)
Toll Free +60 3 3099 4412 (Malaysia)
orders.singapore@partridgepublishing.com

www.partridgepublishing.com/singapore

Preface

The scientific article must be written in a scientific format and may seem confusing for tertiary students and young researchers, especially for the beginning science writer because of its rigid structure, which is so different from writing humanities. One of the reasons for using this format is that it is a means of efficiently communicating scientific findings to a broad community of scientists in a uniform manner.

Perhaps more important than the first is that this format allows the paper to be read at several different levels. For example, many people skim titles to find out what information is available on a subject. Others may read only titles and abstracts. Those wanting to go deeper may look at the tables and figures in the results and so on. The take-home point here is that the scientific format helps ensure that at whatever level a person reads your paper, beyond title skimming, they will likely get the key results and conclusions.

Writing a technical article or research paper is a challenging endeavour for students and young researchers. Publishing your first technical article or research paper requires observation of some essential guidelines.

Hence, the purpose of this book is to provide basic guidelines to tertiary students and young researchers using this user-friendly format to help in writing a scientific article.

This book focuses on the essential steps for the publication of a technical article and research paper for tertiary students and young researchers.

- Laura Cheng

Foreword

In this book, Laura Cheng describes the importance of improving written communication skills for young researchers and tertiary students. Along with thirty-nine short but rich content chapters, permit the reader to know about the role written communication plays in sharing findings and the new knowledge generated as a product of research activities.

Undergraduate students will elaborate on scientific and technical from scholar practices reports, while postgraduate students need to publish their scientific research results in prestigious journals. Millions of papers are published each year, and the number and quality of articles and their citations become a tool for researchers' performance evaluation. Effective communication and specifically the written reports of scientific research results impact the advances in technology, healthcare, political decisions, economic development, and environmental issues, among others, contributing to the welfare of mankind. Anyway, the scientific papers must be written in a language, format, and redaction style that non-expert readers can understand.

The author's focus on young researchers and students has a positive impact on the improvement of their written communication skills for better dissemination of their scientific research results, as it is established in the research life cycle. However, when reading the work, I was able to realise that its content enables us to achieve effective written communication in any field, such as business, politics, public relations, etc. This is also reflected in the writing of the book itself, which, towards the end, grounds knowledge with well-selected examples.

This book is undoubtedly a useful tool for young undergraduate and postgraduate people of the public but also for consolidated researchers or professionals, many of whom ignore small details when writing our articles or scientific reports.

Prof. Benjamin Valdez

Head of the Laboratory of Corrosion and Materials
Autonomous University of Baja California

Developing a communication strategy and formalizing it into a written plan is challenging for most undergraduates and young researchers. *The Essentials for Effective Written Communication for Tertiary Students and Young Researchers* is, indeed, a good guide and useful tool for all young researchers.

The development of a communication strategy and putting it into a written plan is a challenging task for most undergraduates and early career researchers.

There is no doubt that the time and energy invested in this book are well worth it. With a well-configured, tailored strategy and the resultant message platform, everyone within your research organisation can be on the same page in terms of how to communicate your company's mission statement, the underlying reason for its existence, as well as how and why it does what it does.

In her book, Laura Cheng provides the reader with a step-by-step guide to organising your research work as an effective written plan, including "the eight essentials of effective written communication for young scientists and researchers" and additional resources to help you devise an effective communication strategy for navigating a successful future.

I find this book to be an invaluable resource for my faculty library as a professor in the pedagogy department.

Prof. Maria Amparo Oliveros Ruiz

Research Professor Faculty of Pedagogy
Autonomous University of Baja California

About The Author

Laura Cheng Sue Sen is an associate director with an award-winning global public relations firm focused on building influence to deliver impactful communications for business and society.

She graduated from Monash University of Australia with a double major in communications and public relations with distinction and earned a diploma in Industrial Chemistry from the Singapore Polytechnic.

Having worked with government agencies and statutory boards for more than a decade, she has a wealth of experience in business communication and public relations. The experience she gained working for government agencies and statutory organisations gives her an in-depth knowledge of the psychological and social behaviours in society.

She is the lead author for two journals *The Eight Essentials of Effective Written Communication for Young Researchers and Scientists* and *Nine Fundamental Guidelines for Writing a Scientific Article for Publication.*

The success of her published journals made it possible for her to write this book, *The Essentials of Effective Written Communication for Young Scientists and Researchers.*

> *Our learning process is reinforced*
> *by reading and writing.*
> —Laura Cheng

Contents

Chapter 1   An Overview on Communication 1
Chapter 2   Types of Communication 5
Chapter 3   The Benefits of Good Communication Skills ... 12
Chapter 4   Why Young Researchers Should Know about the Importance Publishing Their Work? ... 16
Chapter 5   What Are the Benefits of Scientific Paper Publication for Young Researchers? 20
Chapter 6   The Art of Effective Written Communication 22
Chapter 7   Why It Is Important for Young Researchers to Acquire Good Written Communication Skills? 27
Chapter 8   What Are the Differences in Writing a Technical Article and Research Paper? 31
Chapter 9   An Introduction to Writing a Scientific Journal 35
Chapter 10   Guidelines for Writing the Objectives, Title, and Keywords of a Scientific Research Paper 38
Chapter 11   Guidelines for Writing the Abstract and the Introduction of a Scientific Research Paper ... 43
Chapter 12   Guidelines for Writing the Methodology, Results, Discussion, and Conclusion of a Scientific Research Paper 53
Chapter 13   The Differences between Descriptive and Experimental Research Paper 62

Chapter 14	An Introduction to Effective Written Scientific Communication for Young Researchers and Scientists	65
Chapter 15	The Eight Essentials of Effective Written Communication for Young Scientists and Researchers	70
Chapter 16	What Is a Scientific Research Paper?	84
Chapter 17	An Overview of Research Paper Writing	89
Chapter 18	How to Start Writing a Research Paper?	92
Chapter 19	A Brief Introduction to Digital Publishing Platform for Research Papers	98
Chapter 20	Understanding the Importance of Digital Publishing for Young Researchers	102
Chapter 21	Tips for Choosing the Right Platform for Digital Publishing for Young Researchers	106
Chapter 22	An Overview of How to Publish in a Scientific Journal	110
Chapter 23	An Introduction to Research Paper Types for Undergraduates	118
Chapter 24	A Brief Guide for Writing Analytical Research Papers	123
Chapter 25	A Brief Guide for Writing Interpretation Research Paper	127
Chapter 26	How to Write a Comparative Analysis Paper	130
Chapter 27	Guidelines for Writing Research Report	135
Chapter 28	How to Structure a Research Paper?	139
Chapter 29	Mistakes Young Researchers Make When Writing Literature Reviews	145
Chapter 30	Literature Review Issues and Solutions	149
Chapter 31	Common Mistakes in Scientific Writing	151
Chapter 32	An Overview of Manuscript Language	156
Chapter 33	Mistakes to Avoid in Research	162

Chapter 34 Common Mistakes Made by Young
            Researchers in Laboratory 166
Chapter 35 The Essentials of the Development of
            Writing Skills 170
Chapter 36 The Rationale of Publishing in an
            Academic Journal 174
Chapter 37 What Are the Benefits of Publishing
            Research Findings? 179
Chapter 38 An Introduction to Technical Writing 184
Chapter 39 Researchers' Errors in Journal Compliance 189

Chapter 1

An Overview on Communication

> All creatures on earth require communication with one another. People, on the other hand, are characterised by their ability to use words and language to convey specific meanings.
> —Laura Cheng

Definition for Communication

Communicating involves sending and receiving messages verbally or non-verbally, through speech, oral communication, writing, maps, charts, infographics, and other graphical methods. In the simplest sense, communication is the act of expressing meaning to others.

In his 1992 book, *Communication as Culture*, media critic and theorist James Carey defined communication as a "symbolic process by which reality is created, maintained, repaired, and transformed." Carey argues that we create our reality through sharing our life experiences with others.

It is the nature of all creatures on earth to communicate their feelings and thoughts to one another. Humans, on the other hand, are distinguished from their animal cousins by the ability to use words and language to convey specific meanings.

Aspects of Communication

In any communication, there are two parties involved: a sender and a receiver, a message, and interpretations of meaning on both sides. During and after the message is delivered, the receiver provides feedback to the sender. It is possible to provide feedback in verbal or non-verbal ways, such as nodding in agreement, looking away and sighing, or expressing other emotions or behaviours.

The context of the message, the environment in which it is delivered, and the possibility of interference during transmission or reception must also be considered.

In case the receiver can see the sender, he or she can learn not only the contents of the message, but also the non-verbal signals that the sender is sending out, such as confidence, nervousness, or flippancy. Receivers who can hear the sender will also to understand the sender's tone of voice, such as emphasis and emotion.

Written Communication

The use of writing as a means of communication is another characteristic that sets humans apart from their animal counterparts. It has been a part of human history for more than 5,000 years. As a matter of fact, the first surviving essay, coincidentally about speaking effectively, is thought to date back to around 3,000 BC. It comes from Egypt, though general literacy hadn't been achieved until much later.

As time progresses, this reliance has only grown, especially in the age of the Internet. Nowadays, written communication is one of the primary and most preferred methods of communicating, whether an instant message or a text, a Facebook status, or a tweet.

Messages containing only the written word, such as a text message or e-mail, should be sent with confidence that they are clear and cannot be misinterpreted. It is not considered professional to use emoticons in formal communications to help convey the proper meaning and context of an e-mail without that being the intention of the sender, for example.

Composing Written Communications

If you are preparing a written message, consider your intended audience, the context, and how you intend to deliver it. How can you convey your message effectively? How will you ensure that the message is conveyed correctly? Are there any points that you wish to avoid conveying?

If the subject matter is important and will be conveyed in a professional setting, you may want to proofread the written message, make sure the recipient's name is spelt correctly, and read the message out loud for any dropped words or awkward phrasing before sending it.

> Writing is a skill one must acquire
> as one progresses in society. It comes
> out of your devotion to writing.
> —Laura Cheng

> As one progresses in society, it becomes
> increasingly necessary to acquire writing skills.
> These skills develop from your love of writing.
> —Laura Cheng.

Chapter 2

Types of Communication

> Communication skills are essentials part
> of our personality; it plays a major role
> in the success in all aspects of life.
> —Laura Cheng.

The Importance of Communication

The importance of communication skills is an essential part of our personality. Effective communicators are successful in all aspects of life. An effective presentation demonstrates good communication skills without the need to explain yourself in the future.

Communication comes in a variety of forms, channels, gestures, and expressions, all reflecting what we are feeling and doing. Communication comes spontaneously, but sometimes we may not be fully conscious. Hence, communications can sometimes be misinterpreted or even contradictory because of lack of awareness on our part.

Awareness is paramount to suppressing superlative communication. By staying aware of the subtle signals, we send out every moment, we can align them with what we want to convey. We stop communicating in an accidental manner and become knowledgeable communicators!

> Hyperbolical communication can
> be eliminated by simply being
> aware of what you are saying.
> —Laura Cheng

Different Modes of Communication

It is generally agreed that there are at least five distinct modes of communication: verbal-written, formal, informal, non-verbal, and verbal-oral-face-to-face. With the Internet superhighway offering boundless possibilities, your communication options become practically limitless.

Formal Modes of Communication

Communication of this type is also known as official communication and encompasses all forms of verbal expression that address a formal need.

A predetermined channel is used to conduct it. Among the examples of formal communication are interactions within your profession, scientific communications (laboratory and experimental reports), and analysis documents.

For formal communication, where oral communication is used, such as in meetings or seminars, it is often accompanied by written communication that can serve as documentation evidence of the oral conversation. It could be as simple as the minutes of the meeting or as complex as an in-depth report. In contrast to non-formal communication, it is more time-consuming since it follows a specific protocol.

Our professional lives revolve around formal communication, but not all communication is formal. Expertise in this type of communication is central to professional advancement.

Steps to Improve Your Communication Skills

The following are simple steps to improve your communication skills:

- Clearly state the purpose of your communication.
- Use the same structure, no matter if your expression is oral or written, so that your audience can easily understand it.
- Maintain an open, professional, and friendly tone.

In conclusion, reiterate what you expect this communication to accomplish, such as clarification of your stance, answers to questions, or a call to action. Clarify any restrictions that may apply to this communication, such as confidentiality, deadlines for responses, etc.

As a final note, thank your audience for their attention. It is also applicable to written communication.

Informal Modes of Communication

Informally-communicated information or unofficial information often travels by word of mouth. In this mode of communication, there is no formal structure or procedure. It is free-flowing and spontaneous. Therefore, the information may be less accurate and reliable.

Mostly oral, with no supporting documentation, therefore, many undervalue informal communication, describing it as mere gossip.

Informal communication, despite its disadvantages, is "user-friendly" and, therefore, is extremely beneficial when utilised appropriately.

Communication via Oral Means

The most common form of communication is oral communication. During oral communication, what you express arises from what you say. Likewise, this can be done in formal or informal settings, such as with your family and friends, at a formal meeting or seminar, at work with your colleagues and boss, within your community, during professional presentations, etc.

When you communicate orally, you have the chance to tune, revise, rescind, and correct what you express. As such, it is the most powerful form of communication and can be used to your advantage or disadvantage.

Unlike other forms of communication, oral communication allows you to engage your audience more effectively. With oral communication, audiences often expect you to respond, thus facilitating two-way communication more than any other channel.

What can you do to improve your oral communication?

- You should always look your audience in the eye with confidence, conviction, and openness.
- Make sure your tone and expressions align with the message you wish to convey by practicing in front of a mirror. The tone and expression often convey more than the words themselves.
- Role-playing should be practiced. Even when you are practicing in front of a mirror, you should ask yourself, "Am I receptive to this message with this tone and expression?" If you are not convinced, your audience will not be as well. So practice again until you are comfortable with it.
- Engage your audience in a conscious manner. As a result, don't make your oral expression a one-way rant to yourself. This is the strength of this kind of communication. You can accomplish this by asking questions, obtaining their input, and encouraging them to express their ideas.

Listening as a Skill for Oral Communication

Listen with greater attention. In the case of failure to listen, multiple individuals will attempt to speak at the same time, which undermines the value of this type of communication.

> Active listeners and speakers are
> effective oral communicators.
> —Laura Cheng.

When communicating face-to-face, speak slightly slower. By doing so, you will ensure that you are aware of the subtle nuances in your tone and that the receiver has ample time to comprehend your message.

When you listen, you should always reiterate what you understand. As a result of this type of communication, you miss out on the non-verbal signals, such as anger, friendliness, receptivity, sarcasm, etc., you would see in face-to-face communication. Paraphrase your understanding and confirm that this is, indeed, what the other party was also attempting to convey.

Put on your friendly face with a smile on your lips and eyes when appropriate. Let yourself be friendly. The tone of your voice will automatically convey your openness and receptiveness to the other person. This may not be appropriate if you intend to convey a warning over the phone; therefore, be careful to choose your face according to your message.

Whenever possible, support your remarks with written communication. To ensure everyone is on the same page, it is important to confirm the takeaway from the communication.

It is appropriate to do this even if the call was informal. Perhaps you can send a quick text message to reiterate how enjoyable the conversation was and confirm the final call to action.

> Effective oral communicators listen actively as well as speak.
> —Laura Cheng

Communicating Non-Verbally

There is a more subtle and yet more powerful way to communicate. This includes your physical postures, gestures, tone, and pace of voice, as well as your attitude when you communicate.

The stance you adopt, the hand gestures you display, and other aspects of your physical personality influence how you communicate. Getting up to speed on basic body-language gestures will prevent you from sending mixed messages inadvertently. Make your message more impactful by using this.

The body language you are supposed to adopt sometimes seems in complete contradiction to how you feel; for example, using a friendly posture while feeling threatened or intimidated. When you are consistent in all three aspects—oral, listening, and body language—non-verbal communication will be most effective.

Chapter 3

The Benefits of Good Communication Skills

> Language, if used wisely in communication, has such power over success in all your endeavours.
> —Laura Cheng

Having good communication skills benefits you not only at work but in your personal relationships as well. Whether you are having problems in your personal relationships or at work, lack of communication skills can be the root cause. The benefits of good communication also reflect your confidence; you can make people understand what you want or what message you need.

Being able to communicate fluently and effectively is of great help not only when it comes to ensuring your point is clearly understood but also when it comes to developing confidence in your skills.

In today's workplace and in the personal sphere, good communication is essential for success. Effective communication will improve productivity and relationships in every aspect of a working adult's life.

Listening attentively is essential to effective communication. Empathy, open-mindedness, and constructive feedback are skills. Friendly non-verbal communication, confidence, and a positive demeanour will also help you develop good relationships with your team.

> A crucial part of effective communication is understanding what isn't being said. Understanding what isn't said is therefore necessary.
> —Laura Cheng

The Seven Es and Benefits an Effective Communicator Will Reap

Enhances the Establishment of a Trusting Relationship

Trust is built on effective communication. It helps others trust you when you listen attentively and embrace different points of view. When you act as a role model, this confidence will flow to your team, and they will have confidence in one another.

Enhances the Minimisation of Problems

Communicating well is crucial to resolving conflicts and preventing future ones. Stay calm, make sure all parties are heard, and find a solution that works for everyone.

Enhances Clarity and Direction

If you have effective communication skills, you'll be able to convey clear expectations and objectives to your team. To do this, one needs to find constructive ways to point out when things aren't working as well as provide detailed feedback to get people getting back on track. Having a clear understanding of their specific tasks and responsibilities, as well as those of their teammates, will help eliminate conflicts and confusion.

Enhances the Quality of Relationships

The fact is that good communication also improves your relationships, at work and in your personal life with your friends and family members. Giving people quality feedback and listening carefully help them feel understood and heard. Consequently, this fosters a feeling of mutual respect among people.

Enhances Audience Engagement

People become more engaged with their work when they feel confident in their work and understand what they need to accomplish. According to a recent study on the psychology of employee engagement, less than 15% of employees are satisfied with their employers. When you prioritise effective communication, you will increase team engagement and, thus, boost employee satisfaction.

Enhances Productivity and Efficiency

Team members can focus more on their work when they understand their roles, others' roles, and your expectations. Employees can better manage their workload and conflicts are resolved more quickly with effective communication. This can increase productivity for you and your team.

Enhances the Development of a Team Spirit

Team members who communicate better will be able to rely on one another. Team members won't feel as if they're carrying the whole load. This improved division of labour will lead to better relationships and morale among team members.

Positive work experiences can be nurtured by good communication skills. By listening and understanding people, you naturally improve your work environment.

> Language, if used wisely, has the power
> to make a difference in success.
> —Laura Cheng

Chapter 4

Why Young Researchers Should Know about the Importance Publishing Their Work?

> Young researchers should have a solid
> grasp of the science behind their field
> and know how to communicate it.
> —Laura Cheng

> *While the carpenter does not need to write
> about wood, nor the baker chef about flour,
> the research scientist, unique among trades and
> professions, must provide a written document
> showing what he or she did, why it was done,
> how it was done, and what was learned from it.*
> *—Laura Cheng*

The goal of scientific research is publication, regardless of whether one fully subscribes to the adage "publish or perish." Scientists, starting out as undergraduates, are not measured primarily by their ability to manipulate physical objects in a lab, or by their knowledge of broad or niche scientific fields, and certainly not by their wit and charm, but by their publications.

Young scientists must understand that scientific experiments are not complete until they are published, no matter how spectacular their results may be. A fundamental assumption of science is that original research must be published; only then can new scientific knowledge be authenticated and added to the existing database of knowledge.

While the carpenter does not need to write about wood, nor the baker chef about flour, the research scientist, unique among trades and professions, must provide a written document showing what he or she did, why it was done, how it was done, and what was learned from it.

The scientist must not only conduct science but also write about it. Even though the publication of bad science is not the result of good writing, it is the result of poor writing that prevents or delays the publication of good science. Scientists are often overly committed to their scientific education and training that the communication arts tend to be neglected. Shortly put, many excellent scientists are poor writers. Scientists are often not fond of writing.

> *To be successful as young researchers, they should know the science behind their subjects and know how to present it.*
> —Laura Cheng

Therefore, written communication is crucial. Whether you are writing research journal articles, composing research proposals for funding, or creating a scientific poster to present your work at a conference, written communication is very important.

Besides writing articles for research journals, many scientists in these careers go on to write for popular science magazines, blogs, or answer questions from the public so they have a broad range of audiences and contexts. The ability to articulate groundbreaking research findings to a broad audience is important for them.

The trajectory of their career may be impacted as well. Having the ability to communicate in written form, with not just peers and colleagues, but with government officials, is critical to the implementation of legislation, the dissemination of information about health concerns, and even the shaping of public perceptions of science in many cases.

Communications in science, whether briefings, summaries, articles, or reports, all these cases require that the young scientists know who their audience is as well as the context in which the piece is written.

Each piece must have a purpose. In addition, a person who is working professionally needs to know how to write effectively.

Often this is a non-linear and complicated process. Often you need to work with colleagues in different countries to accomplish your goals. To write journal articles and research proposals, students need to be capable of communicating well. It is also crucial for students to be able to use the appropriate technology to produce, compose, and publish their writing in various settings.

Finding and evaluating relevant sources to use in your written communications is crucial. The sciences are a particularly-collaborative field, and all your work builds on the work of others. To find evidence to support your hypothesis or ideas, you must evaluate, synthesise, and contextualise other people's work. Ultimately, this will enable our young scientists to become effective changemakers, policymakers, and productive citizens in their future careers.

A good way for young scientists to become proficient writers is to write a lot. Taking advantage of outside opportunities to write is also beneficial. A young scientist might write for a club or professional society. Knowing how to communicate effectively means being able to write for a variety of audiences and genres.

> To be a successful researcher, you need
> to publish your scientific findings
> by asking the right question.
> —Laura Cheng

> To be a successful researcher, you must ask
> the right questions to publish your findings.
> —Laura Cheng

Chapter 5

What Are the Benefits of Scientific Paper Publication for Young Researchers?

> The fundamental benefit of
> publishing scientific papers is the
> advancement of knowledge
> —Laura Cheng

It's as important to publish research articles as it is to do the research; disseminating findings is as crucial as the actual findings. These research findings need to be communicated in a manner that can be easily understood and accepted by the target audience. Comprehending the study's highlights and applying writing skills to it will go a long way toward conveying its message.

Postgraduate students, young researchers, and members of the scientific community, whether they are from academia, government, or industry, should equally benefit from all published scientific papers.

A scientific paper publication can have several benefits, including helping you clarify your research goals, assisting you in reviewing and interpreting your own data, as well as forcing you to compare your work with that of others.

Having a scientific paper peer-reviewed provides you with important feedback on the validity of your research approach and can provide insights into how you can advance and interpret your work in the future. The peer-reviewed publication provides evidence to help determine the merit of funding requests for research.

By publishing the research information, you may find other researchers will be able to advance their work, and this will enhance the understanding of your field. When you write and publish a research paper, you put your research in a bigger framework. It helps you establish yourself as an expert in your field.

Publication of a research paper on a particular topic may help the public understand the issue better.

You will be considered for academic appointments as well as promotions if you have a rich body of publications.

> Scientific papers advance knowledge,
> which is the most important
> benefit of publishing them.
> —Laura Cheng

Chapter 6

The Art of Effective Written Communication

Simplify your writing, not the science, when writing a scientific journal, technical article, and a research paper.
—Laura Cheng

What is written communication?

The term written communication refers to any form of communication that is written down. You could write a formal or informal letter, send an e-mail, or anything written. Regardless of what type of writing is used, it should be understood by the target audience.

It's crucial for undergraduates, as well as young scientists and researchers, to have good written communication skills.

Communication styles can be classified based on the tone of the text. There are three major categories: communication written in transactional terms, written communication for information sharing or education, and written directional communication.

Written in Transactional Communication

Writing of this type is a form of communication in which at least two people have involved: the sender and the recipient. In this case, the sender communicates with the receiver to receive a response. Communication takes place in both directions.

Written Information Sharing/ Knowledge Communication

Knowledge communication is the act of communicating information to an audience, regardless of whether the audience subsequently uses the information provided. Information is meant to be made aware to an audience. An advertisement and scientific journals are some of the best examples of this kind of communication.

Written Directional Communication

In this type of communication, the receiver receives specific instructions. Directional communication includes recipes and maps.

In all three types of communication, the main aim is to transfer information from one end to another and assure that the receiver understands what was communicated.

Scientific Journal

Scientific journal is categorised under information sharing/knowledge communication.

Scientific journals often convey messages by using scientific symbols, notation, formulae, etc. for the understanding of their intended audience.

Scientific Symbols

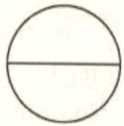

Salt

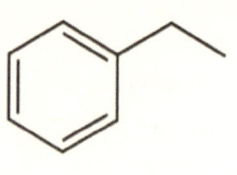   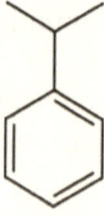   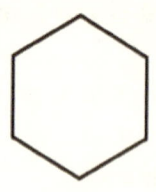

Ethylbenzene   Cumene   Cyclohexane

Scientific Notation

Examples of Scientific Notation

$$45{,}000 \longrightarrow 4.5 \times 10^4$$
$$7.6 \times 10^4 \longrightarrow 0.00076$$

Scientific notation can be used to simplify very large numbers or very small numbers. There is no way we can write such huge numbers on paper, which means the whole numbers can be extended all the way to infinity. In addition, the numbers located at the millions place after the decimal needed to be represented in a simpler way. Therefore, it is difficult to represent a few numbers in their expanded form. Consequently, we use scientific notations.

For instance, 100,000,000, can be written as 10^8, which is the scientific notation. This is a positive exponent. Also, 0.0000001 is a very small number, which can be expressed as 10^{-8}, where the exponent is negative. The above are just examples of scientific notation.

Chemical Formula

The Chemical Formula for Salt - NaCl

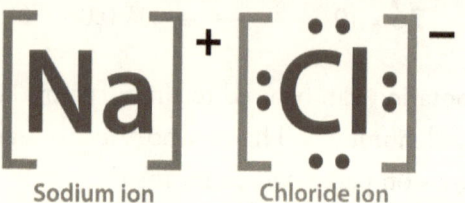

Hydrochloric Acid

The Chemical Formula of Hydrochloric Acid - HCl

$$H^+ - Cl^-$$

The art of effective written communication does not simplify the essence of the subject but rather it simplifies the writing.
—Laura Cheng

Chapter 7

Why It Is Important for Young Researchers to Acquire Good Written Communication Skills?

> *Writing can have a profound impact on many aspects of a researcher's life in the later years of their career, particularly for young researchers.*
> —Laura Cheng

When young researchers publish journal articles or other technical publications on their experiments or research work, it is important for them to acquire good writing skills so their target audience can understand its purpose.

Written communications that do not clearly convey the purpose will be difficult *to understand and may not achieve the purpose.*

Six Key Importance of Written Communication

The importance of written communication can be seen in the fact that it is a form of proof. The publication of a journal constitutes proof or evidence of its existence. To make sure the right intention is conveyed, having good written communication skills is important.

The Use of Voice Modulation and Control Is No Longer Necessary

It is a leading advantage of written communication that the communicator does not need to pay attention to the pitch, tone, or volume of the voice as is the case with oral or verbal communication.

In writing, no such considerations apply. Nevertheless, be aware that writing style may sometimes affect the intention of your communication.

The Opportunity to Edit

Written communication can be proofread many times before it is communicated. This reduces the likelihood of miscommunication. When it comes to oral communication, something said once is already heard and cannot be retracted.

Several real-life examples illustrate how important written communication is in this regard. In open rallies and events, several eminent figures, like politicians and film stars, make controversial oral statements.

Having made these statements, they become controversial, causing people to apologise. The apology is usually made in writing so that it will be on record.

Therefore, it must be clarified that there is no way to revert an oral communication, but written communications can be proofread before publication, so mistakes can be avoided.

Written Communication Does Not Get Lost

Writing is never lost because it is always on the record. The communication could take the form of e-mails, letters, memos, or ads. There will always be a record of written communication. Written communication can always be taken up and referred to in the future. A written communication almost never disappears unless it is deliberately destroyed. That is another advantage of written communication.

Ample Time Is Available

Being convenient, written communication provides ample time for the receiver to read, think, analyse, and then act on the message. This contrasts with oral communication, which almost always requires immediate action. Aside from the fact that written communications allow the receiver ample time to reply, written communication also saves the sender time.

Acts as a Reminder

Documents are physical copies of written communication. For this reason, it serves as a reminder to those who must respond to the communication. The permanence of written communication, as opposed to oral communication that could be forgotten, provides a constant reminder.

The Effectiveness of Written Communication

One of the benefits of written communication is writing is more effective than verbal communication. The likelihood of people believing something written is greater than that of believing something spoken.

> Experiment without a publication
> is just like children at play.
> —Laura Cheng

Chapter 8

What Are the Differences in Writing a Technical Article and Research Paper?

> By being able to distinguish between a technical paper and a research paper, young researchers will be able to provide more relevant titles for their publications.
> —Laura Cheng

Writing research and technical article is a demanding task embroiling several agendum and adjudications. There are differences in writing a technical article and research paper; research paper emphasises the methodology aspect.

What is a research paper?

Research papers are write-ups that record the result/report examinations tired specific zone. For the most part, they take up to this point obscure issues in each field, propose an arrangement for it, and assess the status of the arrangement in comparison with other modern solutions. In this way, in a sense, they move the wilderness of information within the field based on the nature and reason of the movement carried out and the way the write-up is composed.

The research paper involves the study with a clear novel research question and interesting results. It is a full-length, technically-original research document that reports results of major and archival value to the specific community of engineers that comprise the journal audience.

Research papers undergo full peer review. The length of a research paper ranges from 4,000 to 9,000 words with no more than ten figures, whereas a technical article is usually describing a new methodology or presents results from new techniques and should be under 3,000 words with no more than five figures and tables.

What is a technical article?

A technical article is an editorial for a magazine or an Internet benefit that's about a specialised point, and regularly the article drills down into a few low-level details, maybe computers, material science, chemistry, or any other science. It can be around math. It can be approximately pharmaceutical or well-being or diet. It can be around the material science of cooking. There are truly thousands of potential points of specialised articles.

What are the differences between a research paper and a technical article?

The basis of a research paper is more important because it focuses on the fundamentals of an issue. Whereas the objective of a technical article is to focus on the technique angle, not necessarily announce the discoveries.

A senior instructor or educator reviews a research paper before it is submitted. Whereas the author of a technical article does not need an instructor or an educator to review his article.

In a university or college, research papers are usually written by students under the supervision of a professor. Whereas a technical article is a piece that deals with a subject that has been studied or surveyed as of late, written by someone who has expertise in that field.

Even though a research paper may offer a thesis, it is not as in-depth as a thesis paper. Whereas a technical article explores an idea or concept and reports on its effects.

> One of the best ways to upskill one's knowledge is to read relevant technical articles and research papers.
> —Laura Cheng

> Research papers reading is a very important tool to enhance learning from an academic perspective.
> —Laura Cheng

A few of the mechanisms through which professional and academic learning takes place are technical articles and research papers.
—Laura Cheng

Chapter 9

An Introduction to Writing a Scientific Journal

> Scientific journal can be written by all researchers. It is merely gathering all pertinent information and systematically analysing it and putting them down in writing.
> —Laura Cheng

Introduction

The scientific journal must be written in a scientific format and may seem confusing for tertiary students and young researchers, especially for the beginning science writer because of its rigid structure which is so different from writing humanities. One of the reasons for using this format is that it is a means of efficiently communicating scientific findings to a broad community of scientists in a uniform manner.

Perhaps more important than the first is that this format allows the paper to be read at several different levels. For example, many people skim titles to find out what information is available on a subject.

Others may read only titles and abstracts. Those wanting to go deeper may look at the tables and figures in the results and so on. The take-home point here is that the scientific format helps ensure that at whatever level a person reads your paper, beyond title skimming, they will likely get the key results and conclusions.

Hence, the purpose of this chapter is to provide basic guidelines to tertiary students and young researchers using this user-friendly format to help in writing a scientific article.

A guideline is an asseveration by which to ascertain a plan of action. Its purpose is to establish processes according to a set annotation. However, the annotation is just a guideline and is never a requisite.

Scientific journal articles refer to the number of scientific and engineering articles published in the following fields: physics, biology, chemistry, mathematics, clinical medicine, biomedical research, engineering and technology, and earth and space sciences.

Writing a scientific journal is a demanding task embroiling several agendum and adjudications. There are differences in writing a scientific and technical article and research paper; research paper emphasises the methodology aspect.

The research paper involves the study with a clear novel research question and interesting results. It is a full-length technically-original research document that reports results of major and archival value to the specific community of engineers that comprise the journal audience.

Research papers undergo full peer review. The length of a research paper ranges from 4,000 to 9,000 words with no more than ten figures, whereas a technical article is usually describing a new methodology or presents results from new techniques and should be under 3,000 words with no more than five figures and tables.

Sequencing is an essential skill all young researchers must develop if they want to write a good scientific research paper.

> A good scientific research paper
> requires sequence analysis, which is an
> essential skill for all young researchers.
> Throughout the practice of daily
> routines, the idea of chronological order
> is ingrained from an early age.
> —Laura Cheng

Chapter 10

Guidelines for Writing the Objectives, Title, and Keywords of a Scientific Research Paper

> Guidelines serve only to organise all the pertinent information that young researchers have already collected and analysed in a systematic way.
> —Laura Cheng

The concept of chronological order is reinforced from very early on through the practice of the routines of daily life. Similarly, young researchers should be trained to write their papers chronologically at the beginning of their careers.

In this chapter, the essential guidelines for a research paper's objectives, title, and keywords are explained.

Innately, it will be much easier to write the technical article by establishing its objectives. What is my paper about? What are the techniques/designs used? Who/what is studied? What are the results?

The objective of the research paper is the reason given for writing the paper. By stating your objective, you're telling the reader exactly what you're hoping to demonstrate and exactly what they can hope to learn or be convinced of. The objective of a paper is often called a thesis statement, and it needs to be right up front and centre in your paper; if you write it well and give it pride of place in your introduction, then it should give strong support to the rest of your paper.

Objectives and Naming the Title of the Research Paper

Once the objectives are established, a relevant title is easier to be conceived for the technical journal. The title of the technical journal should be more explicit or complete than the evidence permits. This starting point is a very important one because it may influence the impact of your work and the number of readers that it will attract. With the increasing digitalisation of research, more and more people are using abstract databases to find articles relevant to their work.

Your article should begin with a title that succinctly describes the contents of the scientific article paper. Use descriptive words that you would associate strongly with the content of your paper, example the molecule studied, the organism used or studied, the treatment, the location of a field site, the response measured, etc. Most readers will find your paper via electronic database searches, and those search engines key on words found in the title.

The title, abstract, and keywords may well hold an influence on publication accomplishment. It is imperative to get them merited. These three essential elements in the scientific-technical play a decisive role in the elucidation of the scientific and technical article.

Without them, the most scientific-technical article may never be read or even found by interested readers. A good title typically contains 11-14 words, descriptive of terms and phrases that accurately highlight the core content of the paper.

The Importance of a Good Title

The title will be read by many people. Only a few will read the entire paper; therefore, all words in the title should be chosen with care.

The title and abstract are many a time the only parts of a scientific article paper that are unreservedly accessible online. Hence, once readers find your paper, they will read through the title and abstract to determine whether to purchase a full copy of your paper or continue reading.

Most electronic search engines, databases, or journal websites will use the words found in your title and abstract and your list of keywords to decide whether and when to display your paper to interested readers. Thus, these three elements enable the promulgation of your scientific article; without them, readers would not be able to find or cite your paper.

Guidelines for a Good Title

Too short a title is not helpful to the potential reader. However, too long a title can sometimes be even less meaningful. Remember a title is not abstract. Also, a title is not a sentence. Use as few words as possible to describe the content of the paper. Don't use words like "studies on" or "investigations on." Choose specific terms rather than general ones. Be careful with your word order and syntax. Don't use abbreviations or jargon.

Keywords

A keyword is a key to information; it is a tool to help indexers and search engines find relevant papers. If database search engines can find your journal manuscript, readers will be able to find it too.

This will increase the number of people reading your manuscript and likely lead to more citations.

Keywords point researchers to relevant papers—papers that may not come to a researcher's attention in the normal course of her or his reading.

Relevant papers may escape notice because they are published in journals that a particular researcher does not read regularly. And even when such papers are published in journals that the researcher *does* read regularly, he or she may not realise that those papers are relevant because their titles may fail to indicate their relevance. Usually, it consists of four to eight words.

Let us take an example to see why keywords are useful.

For example, a paper titled *Vapour Bio Corrosion Inhibitors (VBCIs) - The Future Trends of Vapour Corrosion Inhibitors (VCIs)* describes that vapour bio corrosion inhibitors will replace the existing traditional VCIs. The title did not mention that it will replace this; however, "future trends," used as keywords, implied that VCIs will be replaced by VBCIs. Suitable keywords like these for such a paper will lead other VCIs researchers to the said paper.

The keywords, title, and abstract of the scientific article operate in a system homologous to a sequence acknowledgement. Once the keywords have assisted people to find the scientific article paper and an effective title has successfully caught and drawn in the readers' attention, it is up to the abstract of the research paper to further generate the readers' interest and maintain their curiosity.

> *Keywords in a research paper are just likened to the power muscles of the journal.*
> *—Laura Cheng*

> *As the journal's power muscles, keywords are the key to a research paper's success.*
> *—Laura Cheng*

> *Research papers that contain keywords are more likely to succeed in journals because they are the muscles of the journal.*
> *—Laura Cheng*

Chapter 11

Guidelines for Writing the Abstract and the Introduction of a Scientific Research Paper

To create an abstract, you need to know what kinds of research papers you will be writing. Abstracts are as diverse as research papers; typically, using an informative abstract is the best approach for young researchers.

> *A journal without a purpose is like*
> *a ship without a rudder.*
> —Laura Cheng

Abstract

The abstract is the first section of your paper that journal editors and reviewers read. In most cases, journal editors and reviewers read the abstract before any other sections of the paper. Reviewers form their initial impressions about your paper by reading your abstract, while busy editors often use it as the decision-making tool to decide whether to send a paper to be peer-reviewed or to reject it outright.

The abstract is one of the essential components of a scientific article. Nevertheless, it can be difficult to specialise an abstract of a scientific article, given that an abstract must be reasonably exhaustive, without giving away too much information. It is primarily because if readers obtain all the details of the scientific article paper in the abstract, they might not read the entire article.

In one paragraph, about 150–250 words long, it summarises the main points of the entire paper in the following prescribed order: the question(s) you investigated (or the purpose); (from introduction) state the purpose very clearly in the first or second sentence, the experimental design, and methods used; (from methods) clearly express the basic design of the study.

Indicate the key techniques used in the methodology without getting carried away with the details. Highlight any key findings (from results). Identify trends, relative changes, differences, etc., and summarise your interpretations and conclusions. Explain what the answers you got from your results mean (from discussion).

The abstract should be written to appeal to the audience of this journal. Do not assume too much or too little background on the topic.

Verify that all information found in the abstract is also included in the paper's body.

The abstract should include all important information of the paper. Whenever possible, avoid citing the introduction as an abstract, using acronyms (spell them out if you must), referencing figures or tables from the body of the paper, using first-person pronouns, or using phrases like "in this paper," "we report," or "will be discussed."

Introduction

Your purpose for writing the paper should be briefly and clearly stated here. In your introduction, you provide the reader with enough background information to understand and evaluate the experiment. Additionally, you explain why this study was conducted.

Among the goals of the introduction is to present the problem and the proposed solution, its nature, and scope; to review the pertinent literature to give the reader a sense of orientation; to set forth the method of experimentation; and to summarise the principal result of the experimentation.

In the introduction, the context of the work being reported is established. This is achieved by discussing relevant primary research literature (with citations) and summarising what we currently understand about the problem you are examining; stating the purpose of your study in the form of a hypothesis, question, or problem you researched; and briefly explaining your rationale and approach and, whenever possible, the possible outcomes of your study.

A good introduction should address the following questions: What was I studying? Why was it an important question? How did we know about it before I did this study? How will this study advance our understanding?

You can think of the introduction as an inverted triangle—the broadest part at the top is the most general information and the narrowest part is the focus on the specific problem.

Introduce the topic by presenting the more general aspects early in the Introduction, then narrow down to the more specific information that provides context, culminating in your statement of purpose and rationale.

To start off on the right foot, sketch out your introduction backwards. Decide what is the specific purpose of your study, and then decide what is the scientific context within which you are asking your question(s).

Once you've determined the scientific context, you'll know what type of general information to include in the introduction.

Here is how information should flow in your introduction:

Begin your introduction by clearly identifying the subject area of interest. Do this by using keywords from your title in the first few sentences of the introduction to get it focused directly on the topic at the appropriate level. This ensures that you get to the primary subject matter quickly without losing focus or discussing information that is too general. For example, from phenomena of corrosion to combating corrosion with environmentally-friendly vapour biocorrosion inhibitors (VBCIs), the words would likely appear within the first one or two sentences of the introduction.

Establish the context by providing a brief and balanced review of the pertinent published literature that is available on the subject. The key is to summarise for the reader what we knew about the specific problem before we did our experiments or studies.

This is accomplished with a general review of the primary research literature, with citations, but should not include very specific and lengthy explanations that you will probably discuss in greater detail later in the discussion.

The judgement of what is general or specific is difficult at first, but with practice and reading of the scientific literature, you will develop a firmer sense of your audience.

Using the mouse behaviour paper as an example, you would introduce the general concept of mating behaviour, then focus on mouse mating behaviours, and then hormonal regulation of behaviour.

Lead the reader to your statement of purpose/hypothesis by focusing your literature review from the more general context (the big picture, e.g., corrosion is a major worldwide problem) to the more specific topic of interest to you (e.g., combating corrosion with VBCIs—vapour bio-based corrosion inhibitors).

What literature should you look for in your review of what we know about the problem? Focus your efforts on the primary research journals—the journals that publish original research articles.

Do not cite sources that contain information that is considered fundamental or "common" knowledge within the discipline, including encyclopedias, textbooks, lab manuals, etc.

Rather, you should cite articles that reported specific results pertinent to your study. Learn how to locate primary literature (research journals) and review articles as soon as possible instead of relying on reference books. Using the references in the literature cited of relevant papers is a good way to move backward in a line of enquiry.

Citation indexes are provided by many academic libraries, allowing researchers to trace a line of enquiry over time. You can get alerts when new papers that cite articles of interest to you are published by some newer search engines. It is particularly useful to review articles because they summarise all the research done on a narrow subject area over a short period (a few years in most cases).

Make sure you clearly state the purpose and hypothesis of your study. When you are first learning to write in this format, it is okay and preferable to use a past statement, like "The purpose of this study was to . . ." or "We investigated three possible mechanisms to explain how VBCI works," etc.

The purpose statement is usually placed near the end of the introduction, often as the topic sentence. If your purpose and expectations are clearly stated, you usually do not need to use words such as "hypothesis" or "null hypothesis."

Clearly explain what your approach is to the problem, for example: state briefly how you approached the problem (e.g., you studied the benefits of vapour bio-based corrosion inhibitors

(VBCIs)). This will usually follow your statement of purpose in the last paragraph of the introduction.

What made you choose this type of experiment or experimental design? Are there any scientific merits to your choice? What advantages does it provide in answering your question(s)?

Do not discuss here the actual techniques or protocols used in your study. This will be done in the materials and methods. Your readers will be quite familiar with the usual techniques and approaches used in your field. If you are using a novel (new, revolutionary, never used before) technique or methodology, the merits of the new technique/method versus the previously-used methods should be presented in the introduction.

This section explains how to write a solid introduction, including background information, the study question, the biological rationale, the hypothesis, and a general approach. You should be able to make it clear to the reader why and on what basis you are positing a particular hypothesis if your introduction is done well.

It begins with a broad question based on an initial observation (e.g., "Many traditional VCI manufacturers developed a wide range of anti-corrosion products to combat corrosion problems at the expense of destroying the environment and endangering the safety of users."). In a scientific paper, it is important to ask broad questions that are not always addressed in the written text.

Understanding the biological rationale for the experiment requires background information, key issues, concepts, terminology, and definitions. Typically, previous relevant studies are summarised. Be concise, cite references, and only include information relevant to your experiment and audience. Using concisely-summarised background information, it is possible to identify specific gaps in scientific knowledge (e.g., "No studies have examined the question of whether environmentally-friendly VBCIs, or vapour bio-based corrosion inhibitors, will represent the future of corrosion inhibitors.).

These are specific, testable questions that address the identified knowledge gap and are much more focused than the broad initial question, for example, "Why are VBCIs, vapour bio-based corrosion inhibitors, environmentally friendly?"

Biological Rationale: describes the purposes of your scientific article, distinguishing what is known and what is not known that defines the knowledge gap that you are addressing.

The biological rationale provides the logic for your hypothesis and experimental approach, describing the biological mechanism and assumptions that explain why your hypothesis should be true.

The biological rationale is based on your interpretation of scientific literature, your personal observations, and the underlying assumptions you are making about how you think the system works.

If you have written your biological rationale, your reader should see your hypothesis in your introduction section and say, "Of course, this hypothesis seems very logical based on the rationale presented."

A thorough rationale defines your assumptions about the system that have not been revealed in scientific literature or from previous systematic observation. These assumptions drive the directions of your specific hypothesis or general predictions.

Defining the rationale is probably the most critical task for the author, as it tells your reader why your scientific article is biologically meaningful.

It may help to think about the rationale as an answer to some questions: How is this investigation related to what we know? What assumptions am I making about what I am yet to know? And how will this experiment add to our knowledge?

There may or may not be broader implications for your study; be careful not to overstate these. Expect to spend time and mental effort on this. You may have to do considerable digging into the scientific literature to define how your experiment fits into what is already known and why it is relevant to pursue.

Be open to the possibility that as you work with and think about your data, you may develop a deeper, more accurate understanding of the experimental system. You may find the original rationale needs to be revised to reflect your new, more sophisticated understanding.

Summary for Writing a Good Scientific Paper in the Introduction

Provide a brief background on the field, why it is important and what has already been achieved, with relevant citations.

Cite a research gap, ask a question, or comment on prior research in this area.

Describe the new aspects of the research and why they are significant.

Don't repeat the abstract, provide unnecessary background information, exaggerate the significance of the work, or claim novelty without a literature review.

> Life is an experiment of endeavours. You must try to acquire the experience.
> —Laura Cheng

> Throughout our lives, we experiment with our endeavours. To acquire experience, you must experiment.
> —Laura Cheng.

Chapter 12

Guidelines for Writing the Methodology, Results, Discussion, and Conclusion of a Scientific Research Paper

> The true value of an experiment lies not only in its conclusion but also in the function of the methodology used.
> —Laura Cheng

How to write the methods section of the scientific research paper?

The purpose of the method section of the journal is to provide sufficient detail so that the experiment can be repeated by competent researchers, though this section will be skipped by most readers because they already know the general methods you used from the introduction. To be considered scientifically valid, your results must be reproducible. Taking this into account, writing this section is important. Taking no such consideration will result in unreliable scientific findings.

A key part of your scientific article is the methodology used.

The methodology describes the broad philosophical underpinning of your chosen research methods, including whether you are using qualitative or quantitative methods, or a mixture of both, and why. Pursuers need to grasp how the data was obtained because the method you chose influences the results and, by extension, how you interpreted their significance.

The methodology is crucial for any branch of scholarship because an unreliable method produces unreliable results and, therefore, undermines the value of your interpretations of the findings.

The process is used to collect information and data for the purpose of writing your scientific article. The methodology may include publication research, interviews, surveys, and other research techniques and could include present and historical information.

Understanding the difference between methods and methodology is of paramount importance. Method is simply a research tool, a component of research, say for example, a qualitative method such as interviews. Methodology is the justification for using a particular research method.

An example is the experimental method; it is an investigation in which a hypothesis is scientifically tested. In an experiment, an independent variable, the cause, is manipulated; and the dependent variable, the effect, is measured; any extraneous variables are controlled. An advantage is that experiments should be objective.

Here are some additional advice on problems common to new scientific writers.

Problem: The methods section is prone to being wordy or overly detailed.

Avoid repeatedly using a single sentence to relate a single action; this results in very lengthy, wordy passages. A related sequence of actions can be combined into one sentence to improve clarity and readability.

Problematic example: This is a very long and wordy description of a common, simple procedure. It is characterised by single actions per sentence and lots of unnecessary details.

> *According to the German VIA Test Method TL 8135-002 test procedure, the Vappro VBCI 10 Foam Emitter was placed in the glass jar. The lid was then covered tightly by turning clockwise. The Vappro VBCI 10 Emitter was placed perpendicular to the base of the jar bottle with all the openings sealed with black duct tape.*

Improved example: Same actions, but all the important information is given in a single concise sentence. Note that superfluous detail and otherwise obvious information has been deleted, while important missing information was added.

> *The Vappro VBCI 10 Emitter was placed in the glass jar with its lid covered and all openings sealed*

> *with duct tape accordingly to the requirements of German VIA Test Method TL8130-02.*

Here, the author assumes the reader has basic knowledge of said German VIA Test Method 8135-002for VCI products, techniques, and has deleted other superfluous information.

Results

The function of the results section is to objectively present your key results, without interpretation, in an orderly and logical sequence using text and illustrative materials (tables and figures).

The results section always begins with text, reporting the key results and referring to your figures and tables as you proceed. Summaries of the statistical analyses may appear either in the text (usually parenthetically) or in the relevant tables or figures (in the legend or as footnotes to the table or figure).

The results section should be organised around tables and/or figures that should be sequenced to present your key findings in a logical order.

The text of the results section should be crafted to follow this sequence and highlight the evidence needed to answer the questions/hypotheses you investigated. Important negative results should be reported too.

Authors usually write the text of the results section based upon the sequence of tables and figures. Avoid providing data that is not critical to answering the research question.

Discussion

Approaches to writing process of the discussion section:

The discussion section provides an immense depiction of viewpoint for readers to remind them of the significance of your study. Discuss your conclusions in order of most to least important. Correlate your results with those from other studies: Are they dependable? If not, discuss possible reasons for the difference.

The purpose of the discussion is to interpret and describe the significance of your findings, considering what was already known about the research problem being investigated, and to explain any new understanding or insights about the problem after you've taken the findings into consideration.

The discussion will always connect to the introduction by way of the research questions or hypotheses you posed and the literature you reviewed, but it does not simply repeat or rearrange the introduction; the discussion should always explain how your study has moved the reader's understanding of the research problem forward from where you left them at the end of the introduction.

Commonly, the section of the discussion should not exceed the epitome of other sections (introduction, material and methods, and results), and it should be completed within six to seven paragraphs. Each paragraph should not contain more than 200 words, and hence, words should be counted repeatedly. The discussion section can be generally divided into three separate paragraphs: (1) introductory paragraph, (2) intermediate paragraphs, and (3) concluding paragraph.

The introductory paragraph contains the main idea of performing the study in question. Without repeating the introduction section of the manuscript, the problem to be addressed and its updates are analysed.

The introductory paragraph starts with an undebatable sentence and proceeds with a part addressing the following questions as (1) On what issue we must concentrate, discuss, or elaborate? (2) What solutions can be recommended to solve this problem? (3) What will be the new, different, and innovative issue? And (4) how will our study contribute to the solution of this problem? An introductory paragraph in this format is helpful to accommodate reader to the rest of the discussion section.

However, summarising the basic findings of the experimental studies in the first paragraph is generally recommended by the editors of the journal.

In the last paragraph of the discussion section, "strong points" of the study should be mentioned using "constrained" and "not too strongly assertive" statements. Indicating limitations of the study will reflect objectivity of the authors and provide answers to the questions that will be directed by the reviewers of the journal. On the other hand, in the last paragraph, future directions or potential clinical applications may be emphasised.

Our access to intermediate paragraphs is using the breakdown tactics. Accordingly, the findings of the study are determined in order of their importance, and a paragraph is constructed for each finding. Each paragraph begins with an "irrefutable" introductory sentence about the topic to be discussed. This sentence basically can be the answer to the question "What have we found?" Then a sentence associated with the subject matter to be discussed is written. Subsequently, in the light of the current literature, this finding is discussed, new ideas on this subject are revealed, and the paragraph ends with a concluding remark.

In this paragraph, main topic should be emphasised without going into much detail. Its place and importance among other studies should be indicated. However, during this procedure, studies should be presented in a logical sequence (i.e., from past to present, from a few to many cases), and aspects of the study contradictory to other studies should be underlined. Results without any supportive evidence or equivocal results should not be written. Besides, numerical values presented in the results section should not be repeated unless required.

In conclusion of the discussion section, using the breakdown tactics remarkably facilitates writing process of the discussion. On the other hand, relevant or irrelevant feedbacks received from our colleagues can contribute to the perfection of the manuscript. Do not forget that none of the manuscripts is perfect, and one should not refrain from writing because of language problems and related lack of experience.

Conclusion

The conclusion of a scientific or research paper is where the writer summarises the paper's findings and generalises their importance. It should end with a well-constructed conclusion. The conclusion is somewhat like the introduction. You restate your aims and objectives and summarise your main findings and evidence for the reader.

Briefly summarise your main points. A good way to go about this is to reread the topic sentence of each major paragraph or section in the body of your paper.

Find a way to briefly restate each point mentioned in each topic sentence in your conclusion. Reinforce the main idea of your essay and leave the reader with an interesting final impression.

Conclusion sections should answer the question "What do your results mean?"

In other words, most of the discussion and conclusion sections should be an interpretation of your results. You should

- Discuss your conclusions in order of most to least important.
- Compare your results with those from other studies: Are they consistent? If not, discuss possible reasons for the difference.
- Mention any inconclusive results and explain them as best you can. You may suggest additional experiments needed to clarify your results.
- Briefly describe the limitations of your study to show reviewers and readers that you have considered your experiment's weaknesses.

Many young researchers are hesitant to do this as they feel it highlights the weaknesses in their research to the editor and reviewer.

However, doing this makes a positive impression of your paper as it makes it clear that you have an in-depth understanding of your topic and can think objectively of your research.

Discuss what your results may mean for researchers in the same field as you, researchers in other fields, and the public. How could your findings be applied?

State how your results extend the findings of previous studies.

If your findings are preliminary, suggest future studies that need to be carried out.

At the end of your discussion and conclusion sections, state your main conclusion once again.

> Experiments are valuable not just
> because of their conclusion but also
> because of the methodology involved.
> —Laura Cheng

Chapter 13

The Differences between Descriptive and Experimental Research Paper

The topics may sound the same, but each research unravels differently.
—Laura Cheng

What is descriptive research?

As a result of its manipulation of variables, descriptive research is commonly used in social sciences to describe phenomena of groups of phenomena. Its main use is gathering information about a population, a situation, or an event. The aim of descriptive research is to collect data and derive insights by using statistical analysis. Among the examples of descriptive research are census statistics as well as survey data.

What is experimental research?

Experimental research refers to research where the researcher manipulates the variable to conclude or finding, and it is difficult to do in social sciences because of manipulating variables. It is useful in finding out the cause-effect of a causal relationship and correlation. Experimental research is also done to this same sort of analysis, but also, it always analyses where the data of an experiment comes from. Example of experimental research includes laboratory experiments.

A Comparison of Descriptive and Experimental Research

The term descriptive research refers to research that describes a phenomenon or a group under study, whereas experimental research refers to research where the researcher manipulates the variable to conclude or finding.

When conducting descriptive research, the researcher observes and describes things, situations, or events. In experimental research, the researcher mainly performs their research in an enclosed environment or laboratory and then results in the best possible outcome.

Descriptive research does not determine the causality of events and, therefore, cannot make predictions about the future. In experimental research, causality is accurately determined, and therefore, predictions can be made.

Descriptive research primarily answers the question "What is?" Experimental research primarily answers the question "What if?"

Studies in sociology and psychology, as well as political science, constitute descriptive research. A typical experimental study may involve a corrosion science, biological study, chemistry, or other laboratory study.

Qualitative and quantitative methods are used in descriptive research.

Experimental research primarily uses quantitative methodology.

The purpose of descriptive research is to collect data and then analyse that data to discover some insight. A similar sort of analysis is conducted in experimental research, but it also always analyses how the data for an experiment came to be.

> Though the research topics are
> similar, there are differences in the
> little details of each study.
> —Laura Cheng

> There may be similarities between the topics,
> but each research unfolds differently.
> —Laura Cheng

Chapter 14

An Introduction to Effective Written Scientific Communication for Young Researchers and Scientists

> *The key to effective writing is to analyse one's audience and purpose.*
> —Laura Cheng

Young scientists and researchers must give talks, write papers and proposals, communicate with a variety of audiences, and educate others. When young scientists and researchers communicate more effectively by giving complete relevant information, science thrives.

Science is increasingly interdisciplinary, and the ability to communicate more effectively across disciplines fosters collaboration and innovation. Being able to communicate the relevance and impact of their ideas and discoveries can enhance scientists' ability to secure funding or find a job.

It allows them to write better and more comprehensible research papers. It also allows them to be better teachers and mentors for next-generation scientists. According to the *Cambridge Dictionary*, communication is the exchange of information and the expression of feeling that can result in understanding, whereas the *Oxford Dictionary* defines communication as the imparting or exchanging of information by speaking, writing, or using some other medium.

Effective written communication is essential for young researchers and scientists because all too often, even a punctuation mark can mean a different meaning to a layperson.

What is written communication?

The written communication is essential and of paramount importance in our daily lives because it is considered more legal and valid than spoken words. Scientific journals, research papers, and research findings all required to be written in formal writings.

Written communication refers to the process of conveying a message, an exchanged between two or among more people, through the use of written symbols.

What is effective written communication?

An effective written communication is a communication between two or among more people wherein the intended message is successfully delivered, received, and understood.

In other words, the communication is said to be effective when all the parties, sender and receiver, in the communication assign similar meanings to the message and listen carefully to what all have been said and make the sender feel heard and understood. In the research world, the communication is effective if the scientific information shared among the field of researchers and contributes to the progress and advancement of science.

Communication covers several other skills, such as non-verbal communication, ability to understand your own emotions, as well as of the other person with whom you are communicating, engaged listening, ability to write clearly and assertively of your scientific finding.

To acquire the skills of effective written communication, young scientists and researchers must know how to convey the intent of your scientific findings explicitly and yet in concise manner, using choicest words that carry maximum impact with examples cited, using of thesaurus to avoid the usage of repetitive words, proper usage of punctuation marks, and the importance of paragraphing. It by no means advocates eliminating the crucial means of verbal communications and personal interaction.

Knowing what's essential is the key to understanding what's important and what's not for an effective written communication.

What is scientific written communication?

The written communication among researchers and scientists is a process wherein the written message in the form of scientific ideas, thoughts, and opinions are transmitted between two or among more people with the intent of creating a shared understanding.

The written communication is the most common and effective mode of communication. In any research organisation, the electronic mails, memos, reports, documents, letters, journals, job descriptions, employee manuals, etc. are some of the commonly-used forms of written communication.

Written communication provides a more permanent record and can avoid misunderstandings.

The effectiveness of written content depends on the correct choice of words, their organisation into correct sentence sequence, and the cohesiveness in the sentences.

The information in writing is considered more legal and valid than the spoken words. Also, people rely more on the written content than what has been said orally. But however, unlike verbal communication, the feedback of written communication is not immediate since it is not spontaneous and requires time to get into the understandable form.

There are several factors involved in effective written communication; however, only the eight essentials of effective written communication will be discussed in the next chapter of the book.

Many of the problems that occur in the research organisation are the direct result of young scientists and researchers failing to communicate or communicating ineffectively of their research findings.

An effective communicator not only thinks about what to say, but also how to say it. To communicate effectively, it is not enough to have well-organised ideas expressed in complete and coherent sentences and paragraphs. One must also think about the style, tone, and clarity of his/her writing and adapt these elements to the reading audience.

> *Understanding essentials of writing a scientific journal gives you an insight and understanding of what is important and what is unnecessary.*
> *—Laura Cheng*

> *Understanding essentials is the key to understanding what is important and what isn't for effective written communication.*
> *—Laura Cheng*

Chapter 15

The Eight Essentials of Effective Written Communication for Young Scientists and Researchers

> *It is important to understand essentials to identify what is important and what isn't when writing a scientific journal.*
> —Laura Cheng

First Essential - Lucid

Writing clearly and concisely means choosing your words or scientific term deliberately, constructing your sentences carefully, using grammar properly. By writing clearly and concisely, you will get straight to your point in a way your audience can easily comprehend.

The written message should be clear and easily understandable to all your recipients; hence, avoid using jargons, acronyms when communicating with lay people.

Using jargon when communicating with laypeople can be the worst form of communication. Jargon is the technical terminology or characteristic idiom of a special activity or group. It's any word or phrase that loses or changes meaning when you use it with people who aren't in your field.

Most audiences don't respond well to jargon. Even with explanation, your audience will likely be less engaged to your written communication. When communicating with laypeople, plain English is fundamental to clear effective written communication; it helps make things clear, simple, and quick to understand; hence, avoid using acronyms as well.

The purpose of the written communication should be clear to sender, then only the receiver will be sure about it. The message should emphasise on a single goal at a time and shall not cover several ideas in a single sentence.

Second Essential - Precise Language

Ambiguity creates confusion, fear, stress, and resistance. Make it a point to be clear, crisp, concise when you write. Embrace clarity; it will serve you well. The written message should be precise, i.e., a correct language should be used, and the sender must ensure that there are no grammatical and spelling mistakes. Also, the message should be exact and well-timed. The correct messages have a greater impact on the receiver, and at the same time, the morale of the sender increases with the accurate message.

To choose the most effective language, the writer must consider the objective of the document, the context in which it is being written, and who will be reading it. Precision in language includes descriptions that create tangible images with details the reader can visualise. Abstract language is vague and obscure and does not recall specific visual images.

Consider the two sets of statements below.

The statement 1 is abstract and vague, whereas the statement 2 is precise and leaves no ambiguity.

Statement 1: *"Professor John, my research paper will be ready next week."* Which day would you be expecting the research paper to be ready? It will be interesting to see different people's interpretation of the timing phrase "next week" as day varies. It could range from Monday to Friday. The said statement is vague and ambiguous.

Statement 2: *"Professor John, my research paper will be ready next Tuesday by 10:00 a.m."* Statement 2 involves the actual day and time; you can expect him to submit his research paper on Tuesday by 10:00 a.m. Statement 2 involves the usage of precision in language.

Third Essential - Complete

Your written message should be complete, i.e., it must include all the relevant information as required by the intended audience. The complete information gives answers to all the questions of the receivers and helps in better understanding by the recipient.

Scientists and researchers must give talks, write papers and proposals, communicate with a variety of audiences, and educate others.

When scientists and researchers communicate more effectively by giving complete relevant information, science thrives; science is increasingly interdisciplinary, and the ability to communicate more effectively across disciplines fosters collaboration and innovation.

Being able to communicate the relevance and impact of their ideas and discoveries can enhance scientists' ability to secure funding or find a job. It allows them to write better and more comprehensible research papers. It also allows them to be better teachers and mentors for next-generation scientists.

When scientists can communicate effectively beyond their peers to broader non-scientist audiences, it builds support for science, promotes understanding of its wider relevance to society, and encourages more-informed decision-making at all levels, from government to communities to individuals. It can also make science accessible to audiences that traditionally have been excluded from the process of science.

Hence, effective written communication can help make science more diverse and inclusive.

Fourth Essential - Specific

The communication should be specific; it should be clear and leaves no room for misinterpretation. All the scientific facts and figures should be clearly mentioned in a message.

Use appropriate specific language because the meaning of words can be relative and situational.

Words can be interpreted in different ways by different people in different situations.

It is important to choose language that is as precise, specific, and clear as possible to eliminate number of possible interpretations for a message.

Consider the following statements:

For example: *"Is the pH meter an expensive laboratory equipment?"* It is best answered with a comparison: *"Compared to that of a gas chromatography, the pH meter is not an expensive laboratory equipment."*

When the message is specific, it will eliminate the misinterpretation of what an expensive laboratory equipment is as compared to the gas chromatography.

Would other people consider a pH meter an expensive laboratory as compared to gas chromatography? In actuality, the range of values varies greatly because the question "Is pH meter an expensive laboratory equipment?" is relative; they can mean different things to different people in different comparisons. Hence, using precise and specific language is essential to effective communication.

Fifth Essential - Concise

Keep sentences short and concise. Leave out words that do not contribute to the main focus of the communication. The message should be precise and to the point.

The sender should avoid the lengthy sentences and try to convey the subject matter in the least possible words. The short and brief message is more comprehensive and helps in retaining the receiver's attention. Less is more when it comes to length.

Leave out words that do not contribute to the focus of the communication. Avoid information that is not relevant.

Clarity is key.

Statements 2 and 4 below show examples on how to keep your message short and concise without leaving the essence of your message.

Example, statement 1: *"Professor John, I will be bringing fried chicken wings seasoned with salt and coarse black pepper. It will be fried with oil and will be packaged in silver metal container for our new science students' gathering."*

Statement 2: *"Professor John, I will be bringing fried black pepper chicken wings for our new science students' gathering."*

Statement 1 involves the usage of redundant words, such as "fried with oil." What do you fry the chicken with? *Needless to say with oil.* "Packaged in silver metal container." Isn't silver metal? *Needless to say, it is metal.*

Statement 2 focuses only on "fried black chicken wings for our new science students," which is the main focus of the communication, and it avoided lengthy sentences in conveying the subject matter.

Statement 3: *"I am contacting you with regard to the position of a lecturer advertised by the university in the newspaper last Sunday."*

Statement 4: *"I am writing about the position of a lecturer you advertised."*

The essence of your writing is to let the advertiser know that you are responding to his advertisement. Hence, statement 4 is precise and to the point, which is the essential to effective written communication.

Sixth Essential - Paragraphing

Paragraphs help organise a text and give it structure. They are like mini texts, expressing a complete idea in a few sentences. Effective written communication for technical reports, academic or journal writing, involves writing in paragraphs; it serves as building blocks to construct a complex analysis or argument. Paragraphing helps readers understand and process your ideas into meaningful units of thought.

The process involving paragraphing can be divided into three segments:

Topic Sentence

The topic sentence is the focus of the paragraph. If the paragraph is part of an essay, the topic sentence is not only the focus the paragraph, but it supports the thesis as well. This sentence is your main idea, and all other sentences included in this topic sentence must fit under its umbrella.

Example of a topic sentence on "technology":

Sentence 1: *"Technology has enhanced my everyday learning by richly improving each learning opportunity."*

Sentence 2: *"Technology has enhanced my everyday learning by richly improving each learning opportunity by using a computer."*

Sentence 1 supports the topic sentence on the subject on enhanced learning through "technology" and how it has enhanced your learning opportunity, but it does not provide specific information what types of technology help in your enhanced learning.

Sentence 2 supports the topic sentence on the subject enhanced learning through "technology" and provides the types of technology involved as well.

This supports the topic sentence and provides specific information. Ultimately, technology, such as a computer, provides enhanced learning opportunity, and it gives a sense of completion.

Supporting Details

Develop your paragraph with supporting details. You can further break down this step into examples and explanation. Also, notice "details" is plural. Two examples are always better than one. For each example that you provide, you will want to explain how it supports your topic sentence.

Transition Sentences

It guides your reader smoothly from the topic of the preceding paragraph into the topic of your new paragraph. Writers sometimes begin with a transition sentence before introducing the topic of the new paragraph. The most basic transition words are conjunctions that join words, phrases, or clauses together.

For example, words like *and*, *but*, and *or* can connect two sentences together.

The two sentences below show how conjunctions effectively connect two sentences together.

"I worked 'til 11:00 p.m. yesterday, and I managed to finish my math assignment."

"I worked 'til 11:00 p.m. yesterday, but I was still not able to finish my math assignment."

Concluding or Transitional Sentence

Depending on the purpose of your paragraph, you will either write a concluding sentence or a transitional sentence. If your paragraph is part of a whole essay, you will write a transitional sentence that links to the next paragraph. Transition words and sentence help make a piece of writing flow better and connect one idea to the next. Because there's more than one way to connect ideas, there are many types of transitional phrases to show a variety of relationships. Some words will help you show the order in which events occur, while others explain a cause-and-effect relationship or allow you to present your ideas in a hierarchy of importance.

If you are writing only a paragraph, your last sentence is a true concluding sentence. In both instances, the concluding sentence should give a sense of completion by drawing together the support to emphasise your focus or topic sentence.

Seventh Essential - Punctuation and Grammar

Punctuation and correct grammar are keys to effective written communication Punctuation is the use of special marks to enable readers to understand a piece of writing. Good punctuation follows the rhythms of speech, telling the reader to pause at the right points and to organise the information in the document that he or she is reading. It reduces misunderstanding and makes the writing clear.

Correct grammar, punctuation, and spelling are keys to good written communication. The reader will form an opinion of the author based on the content and presentation, and errors are likely to lead them to form a negative impression.

All written communications should, therefore, be reread before sending to print or hitting the send button in the case of e-mails, as it is likely that there will be errors. Do not assume that spelling and grammar checkers will identify all mistakes as many incorrect words can indeed be spelt correctly (for example, when *advice* is used instead of *advise* or *principle* instead of *principal*.

Advice is a noun, meaning an opinion or recommendation offered as a guide to action, conduct, etc; while *advise* is a verb, meaning to give counsel to, offer an opinion or suggestion as worth following.

Principal can also be used as an adjective, meaning first or highest in rank, importance, or value, as in the principal objective of this article is to teach you the difference between two words. *Principle*, on the other hand, is a rule of action or conduct or a fundamental doctrine or tenet.

If possible, take a break before rereading and checking your writing, as you are more likely to notice problems when you read it fresh.

Eighth Essential - Courtesy

Courtesy in written communication implies being respectful of the recipient's culture, values, and beliefs. Also, it involves the need to adopt a register your audience can easily relate to and understand. Courteous communication has a positive impact on the overall written communication, as it prompts a more positive and constructive approach to the conversation.

When we meet people face-to-face, we use the other person's body language, vocal tone, and facial expressions to assess how they feel. However, in written communication, we can't tell when people have misunderstood our messages.

Hence, our choice of words, sentence length, punctuation, and capitalisation can easily be misinterpreted without visual and auditory cues. In the first example below, Emma might think that Harry is frustrated or angry, but in reality, he feels fine.

Tone in writing can be defined as attitude or emotion towards the subject and the reader; if used correctly, it helps your writing be more effective. Certain forms of communication, like memorandums and proposals, need a formal tone.

Writing to someone you know well would need a more informal tone. The kind of tone depends on the audience and purpose of the writing. It implies that the sender must take into consideration the feelings and viewpoints of the receiver, such that the message is positive and focused on the audience. The message should not be biased and must include the terms that show respect for the recipient.

How to write an effective conclusion for your scientific journal?

A hallmark of effective written communication is having the ability to express the desired message in as few words as possible. Good scientific writers, in other words, use language which is straightforward and to the point.

Writing a scientific or research paper conclusion is where the writer can summarise the paper's findings and generalise their importance. It should end with a well-constructed conclusion. The conclusion is somewhat like the introduction. You restate your aims and objectives and summarise your main findings and evidence for the reader.

Briefly summarise your main points; a good way to go about this is to reread the topic sentence of each major paragraph or section in the body of your paper.

Find a way to briefly restate each point mentioned in each topic sentence in your conclusion. Reinforce the main idea of your essay and leave the reader with an interesting final impression.

Conclusion sections should answer the question "What do your results mean?"

In other words, most of the discussion and conclusion sections should be an interpretation of your results. You should

- Discuss your conclusions in order of most to least important.
- Compare your results with those from other studies: Are they consistent? If not, discuss possible reasons for the difference.
- Mention any inconclusive results and explain them as best you can. You may suggest additional experiments needed to clarify your results.
- Briefly describe the limitations of your study to show reviewers and readers that you have considered your experiment's weaknesses.

Many researchers are hesitant to do this as they feel it highlights the weaknesses in their research to the editor and reviewer. However, doing this makes a positive impression of your paper as it makes it clear that you have an in-depth understanding of your topic and can think objectively of your research.

Discuss what your results may mean for researchers in the same field as you, researchers in other fields, and the public.

How could your findings be applied?

State how your results extend the findings of previous studies.

If your findings are preliminary, suggest future studies that need to be carried out.

At the end of your discussion and conclusions sections, state your main conclusion once again.

The said eight essentials of an effective written communication will serve young scientists and researchers well in writing their scientific reports or journals.

> *Identifying what is important and what isn't requires understanding essentials.*
> —*Laura Cheng*

Chapter 16

What Is a Scientific Research Paper?

> In short, research paper is simply the
> process of researching, analysing,
> thinking, and putting down all the
> data of a research topic in writing.
> —Laura Cheng

A scientific research paper is any piece of article writing in which the writer must research a topic in depth. Scientific research papers are based on facts rather than opinions and are written from the point of view of the author.

It requires the author to form an opinion on the topic, gain expertise on the subject, and back up their conclusions and assertions with evidence gathered through thorough research.

In another definition, a scientific research paper is an extended essay that presents your own interpretation or evaluation. In your essay, you incorporate all the knowledge and experience you have regarding a subject.

Objectives

The main objective of a scientific research paper is to build upon what you already know and to seek out opinions from experts. The goal of a research paper is to find the best possible information about a certain field of knowledge. Knowing how to approach a survey can make it orderly and focused. Despite the sea of sources, you won't get lost.

What is the process?

The process of researching, analysing, thinking, and writing a scientific research paper is time-consuming. Scholars seek information to expand, use, verify, or deny findings when they are looking for answers to questions.

A research paper is a product of considering writing works and following specific requirements to produce it. Additionally, scientists develop technological or social aspects of human science by researching and progressing many theories.

To write relevant papers, however, they must understand the research, its structure, characteristics, and types.

Are there different types of research papers?

There are several different types of research papers. Each type of research paper requires different preparation, so it is important to know what is required for your assignment.

There are several common types of research papers, including analytical approach, persuasive approach, definition approach, comparative approach, interpretative approach, experimental approach, etc. In this chapter, we will only focus on the said types of research papers.

Analytical Approach Research Paper

An analytical research paper combines a question with relevant data collected from other researchers to identify their differences and similarities. Research is about finding out what other researchers have discovered and making personal conclusions about the topic. It is essential to remain neutral and not voice your own negative or positive opinion on the issue.

Persuasive Approach Research Paper

Within a single paper, the persuasive paper presents both sides of a controversial issue. Its goal is to convince the reader to agree with your point of view. There should be a discussion of both sides of the issue and citations of different researchers, but the author should favour one side over the other and try to convince the reader to support the side they favour. Despite this, your arguments should be logically founded and backed up by statistical data and facts.

Definition Approach Research Paper

Definition papers merely present facts or objective arguments without including an author's opinion or feeling. They serve merely as sources of information. It is important to include information from multiple sources, but it should not be analysed.

Comparative Approach Research Paper

Studies that compare two viewpoints, authors, or subjects are known as comparative research papers. In your paper, make sure both sides are adequately described before comparing them and deciding which one to support.

Interpretative Approach Research Paper

When writing an interpretive paper, you must use the knowledge you have gained from your research, for example, from a case study in law. To support your statement and conclusion, make sure you back them up with valid data and an established theoretical framework.

Experimental Approach Research Paper

Basically, such a paper describes in detail a particular experiment. This happens most often in the fields of biology, chemistry, and physics. Experiments attempt to explain a phenomenon or outcome with specific actions. The data supporting your experiment must be presented and analysed thoroughly.

Adhering strictly to one form of
writing of scientific journals stiffer
the creativity of science.
—Laura Cheng

Scientists cannot be creative if they
adhere to one form of writing for
different topics of their subjects.
—Laura Cheng

Chapter 17

An Overview of Research Paper Writing

> To continue to advance in our fields of expertise and broaden our minds, we must continue to conduct research.
> —Laura Cheng

What is a research paper?

Research papers are common forms of academic writing. To write a research paper, a student or academic must find information on a topic (that is, conduct research), take a position on that topic, and provide evidence or support for that position.

Researchers may also refer to research papers as scholarly articles that contain the results of their own original studies or evaluate other studies. Prior to being accepted for publication in an academic journal, scholarly articles are often peer-reviewed.

The Purpose of a Research Paper

Researchers, students, academics, or people of any background can conduct detailed studies on certain topics related mostly to technology as a *proof of concept*. In this paper, we show how some tasks can be accomplished on a preliminary basis.

For example, you may read existing papers on the efficacy of vapour corrosion inhibitors (VCIs) and how they work, and upon that existing work, you propose a more concrete solution to the vapour corrosion inhibition theory by conducting an experiment to validate its claims.

How should a research paper be written for maximum effectiveness?

For maximum effectiveness, a research paper should include a title, the name/s of author/s, abstract, introduction, related work, proposed methodology, approaches, conclusion, and references.

Title: A font such as Times New Roman is preferred for the title of the research paper. It should be placed near the top of the document in the centre.

Author/s name/s: You will find the name/s in a row beneath the title. You can also list down authors' names or separate it by commas if there are multiple authors and the names do not fit in the row.

Abstract: It describes the overall theme, content, or idea of your research paper.

Introduction: It describes your research and how you propose to proceed, probably for what you are most proficient at, such as proposed system or approaches.

Related work: It discusses the successes and failures of what has been done in the field so far, discusses which research papers were produced by which authors.

Proposed methodology or proposed work: This is the most crucial section. An easy-to-understand language in a highly-technical area is the best choice. The purpose of this section is to describe what you see as the research's value-adding idea and what should be done to add to it.

Approaches: Once again, this is one of the crucial sections. Your proposal should explain how it works. If you propose an algorithm, for example, can you explain how it works? Include an example of the algorithm. This is like a section on the practicalities of your paper.

Conclusion: There are some points or upcoming technologies or approaches you can list here. You should end your paper with a proper conclusion and then reference some work from the field that you believe may be of use in the future.

References: This is an essential section. In this section, you can list, chronologically and with numbers any references to existing research papers as well as website links.

> A research paper's guide provides a
> highly-developed values system that
> acts as a compass. If you find yourself
> lost while writing your paper, it
> points you in the right direction.
> —Laura Cheng

Chapter 18

How to Start Writing a Research Paper?

> A guide is a highly-developed values system, like having a compass in your hand. Whenever you are lost, you can use it as a guide to get you back on track.
> —Laura Cheng

All young scientists must be familiar with research papers, right? All of them will eventually write one. It is likely that they will come across questions like, "What approaches should I take in writing a research paper?" or "What should I include in my research paper?" and many others. This chapter will discuss all aspects of composing a research paper.

Let's start by defining what exactly a research paper is. A research paper is a piece of writing written by students, professionals, or others with an in-depth study of a topic. Writing a research paper is not a task that can be completed in a few days. The process involves a lot of research and study. The skills that you acquire while writing a research paper will be very useful to you as you progress in your career.

Some Methods for Writing a Strong Research Paper

Topic selection: Before beginning a research paper, it is important to select a topic. You can come up with various topics and can choose one based on its relevance to you. You can start by asking yourself many questions, such as *Am I comfortable in this field?* Or *am I able to do deep research on this subject?* Or *what innovative ideas can I contribute to this field?*

If you receive a positive response, you should choose that topic. It is also important to discuss the topic with your mentors and guides to learn whether it is worthwhile.

Focus on a topic: You should check whether a topic is specific or general after choosing it. The topic should be narrowed down if it is very broad since the research paper must be more topic-specific than generic. Consult your mentor for more information.

Information gathering: *This is a crucial step! Before you begin your research study, you* must gather information. The Internet is the best source of information in today's era. The Internet provides a lot of information, but not all of it is reliable, so you must check out a variety of sources. Research strategies must focus on specific directions and meet the required objectives. There are various other sources from where you can get the relevant information as you can discuss it with your mentors, study the journals, etc.

Preparation of information by filtering and drafting: By the time you have gathered all the information about the topic, you will have a lot of information. To filter out information, you must deeply analyse it. If you are writing a genuine research paper, you should avoid all the irrelevant details. Following filtration, it is necessary to organise all the information and come up with a final draft, which may be formal or informal. In the drafting process, all aspects are considered, such as information accuracy, spelling errors, unnecessary information, etc. Make sure the content is relevant to the topic by proofreading it once.

The gathered information now needs to be compiled into the research paper outline, which consists of

Title: Once the objectives are established, a relevant title is easier to be conceived for the technical journal. The title of the research paper should be more explicit or complete than the evidence permits. This starting point is a very important one because it may influence the impact of your work and the number of readers that it will attract. With the increasing digitalisation of research, more and more people are using abstract databases to find articles relevant to their work. For any kind of content, besides the research paper, the title is what attracts the readers' attention. Many times a person decides whether to read an article by just looking at its title. A good title should be very catchy and informative. The objective of the paper must be summed up in a few words. The average length of a title is around 20 words. In addition, you should avoid unnecessary terms from the title, such as the likes of "Research on . . ." or "Paper on . . ."

Abstract: Abstracts are like summaries of your research. By describing briefly, the key findings of the research paper, it helps the reader gain a better understanding of the research paper. About 300–350 words would be ideal.

Keywords: A keyword is a key to information; it is a tool to help indexers and search engines find relevant papers. If database search engines can find your journal manuscript, readers will be able to find it too. This will increase the number of people reading your manuscript and likely lead to more citations. Keywords point researchers to relevant papers—papers that may not come to a researcher's attention in the normal course of her or his reading. Relevant papers may escape notice because they are published in journals that a particular researcher does not read regularly. And even when such papers are published in journals that the researcher *does* read regularly, he or she may not realise that those papers are relevant because their titles may fail to indicate their relevance. Usually, it consists of four to eight words.

Introduction: The function of the introduction is to establish the context of the work being reported. This is accomplished by discussing the relevant primary research literature, with citations, and summarising our current understanding of the problem you are investigating; stating the purpose of the work in the form of the hypothesis, question, or problem you investigated; and briefly explaining your rationale and approach and, whenever possible, the possible outcomes your study can provide. The introduction must contain adequate information about the topic, which describes in detail the purpose of your study. In this section, the topic should be clearly explained as well as the reason for studying it. You should also explain why your research paper is worth reading for the readers. Pay attention to spelling and grammar and ensure your sentences and phrases are simple and accurate.

Proposed methodology or proposed work: This section is the core of the research paper as your actual study work, research findings, methodologies, approaches, and all are stated here. Be specific about your topic and try to avoid unnecessary information. You can use tables, flowcharts, pie charts, etc. to show statistics.

Results: All your research results are listed in the results section. Throughout this section, all the outcomes of the research process are detailed and noted. Present the results of your research in the form of tables, graphs, or charts after analysing and filtering the data. According to the rest of the sections, this section can be varied in length.

Conclusion: What you have stated in the introduction section has to be described in the conclusion section; it must be explained how you achieved it based on the results of the research study and methodologies, which you have already specified under the results section. Your conclusion summarises the results of the research study.

Discussion: The discussion section provides an immense depiction of viewpoint for readers to remind them of the significance of your study. Discuss your conclusions in order of most to least important. Correlate your results with those from other studies: Are they dependable? If not, discuss possible reasons for the difference.

The purpose of the discussion is to interpret and describe the significance of your findings, considering what was already known about the research problem being investigated, and to explain any new understanding or insights about the problem after you've taken the findings into consideration. The discussion will always connect to the introduction by way of the research questions or hypotheses you posed and the literature you reviewed, but it does not simply repeat or rearrange the introduction; the discussion should always explain how your study has moved the reader's understanding of the research problem forward from where you left them at the end of the introduction.

Recommendation: It is not mandatory to include this section in your research paper, and it is created according to its relevance and requirements. Whatever you mention in this section, it must be logical and based on your research. This section does not allow you to throw anything into it that you think might be useful.

References: This section is crucial. References and website links to existing research papers can be listed chronologically and numbered in this section.

> To broaden our minds and excel
> in our fields of expertise, we must
> continue to carry out research.
> —Laura Cheng

Chapter 19

A Brief Introduction to Digital Publishing Platform for Research Papers

> Young researchers who comprehend the
> importance of choosing the right platform
> for their research paper are more likely
> to choose the most suitable platform
> for publishing their manuscripts.
> —Laura Cheng

After you have completed your research paper, you need to publish it. Today digital publishing platforms are created to allow researchers immediate access to the things they are interested in reading.

What is digital publishing platform?

Digital publishing platforms allow you to publish longer texts, or graphic-focused editions, such as catalogues or albums, in a digital form, accessible via any electronic device, such as a computer, tablet, or smartphone.

What is digital publishing?

Typically, digital publishing means a book or manuscript won't be printed but instead will be available digitally, like in an e-book or e-copy of a research paper. There is the option of printing on demand for researchers or readers.

Among most researchers today, digital publishing has become increasingly popular. It is up to each researcher to decide what their career and life goals are. Many authors, however, do both!

What are the advantages of digital publication?

Digital articles can also be stored in a smaller space than traditional hardcovers and paperbacks. Additionally, having so many books available wherever you are and wherever you have your reading device is convenient; it's much easier to take a phone or a Kindle on a vacation than ten physical books.

Traditional publishers may not be able to get your book to you as fast as you'd like. Most traditional publishers require submissions to be represented/agented, but many digital publishers will accept un-agented submissions.

Even though digital publishers may not be able to get your book into bookstores, they do provide the ability to purchase your book online.

Readers can now access your book or research articles no matter where they are and how much time it takes to deliver. So even if they can't get to a bookstore or don't want to wait, they can still get it.

Visual content dominance—digitalisation's popularity is on the rise. There is a rise in visual stimulation. According to 80% of businesses surveyed in 2020, 46% of marketing will be done using visuals. According to TechCrunch, visual content creation and consumption have increased by 842% since early 2016.

A website or media channel with visual content will encourage readers to spend more time on the site. Additionally, it's essential for driving emotions and motivating audiences to act.

Huge Cost Savings

By using a digital publishing platform, you can accomplish just that. You could dramatically reduce publishing costs if you reduced or eliminated print media.

Furthermore, you can have a positive impact on the environment. You don't have to print your magazine, thereby reducing the demand for paper.

Don't forget that when it comes to digital self-publishing, you are responsible for quality control. Other benefits of digital publishing are a broader range of books and no costs or lower operating costs.

Researchers need to do their homework to figure out if digital publishing is right for them and, if so, which publisher or platform is best for their needs.

> Digital boundaries are becoming
> more fluid, resulting in the emergence
> of a new kind of literacy.
> —Laura Cheng

Chapter 20

Understanding the Importance of Digital Publishing for Young Researchers

Print publishing is rapidly being overtaken by digital media. In the aftermath of the COVID-19 outbreak, publishers have rushed to increase their online distribution and diversify their revenue models, which has accelerated the rise of digital media.

> Eventually, the convenience of
> e-publication will replace the nostalgia
> of traditional book publishing.
> —Laura Cheng

The Demand and Rise of Digital Publication

Publishing digitally continues to expand and grow. In 2018, e-book sales accounted for 25% of all book sales, up from 12% in 2013.

The *Financial Times* and the *New York Times* have more digital subscribers than print subscribers, and even local newspapers like the *Boston Globe* have a larger digital audience than print subscribers.

Apart from digital subscriptions, artificial intelligence in publishing and content categorisation are two of the most important trends in digital publishing today

The Benefits of Digital Publication of Your Research Paper

Your research paper is always accessible at the fingertips of your readers on a digital publishing platform, 24 hours a day, seven days a week. You can also reach a global audience.

Young researchers benefit from the online publishing industry in several ways. The other advantage of e-books, for example, is that they don't have to adhere to the length restrictions that exist in traditional publishing. Typically, novels range from 40,000 to more than 300,000 words but rarely go beyond or below these numbers because of the high cost of printing. However, e-books can be, if the author deems necessary. As a result, writers and publishers have access to a wide variety of possibilities.

When publishing print magazines, publishers must determine how best to integrate advertisements into the content. In contrast, digital journals do not have length restrictions on publishers. This new freedom has made it possible to experiment with new formats.

A digital media publisher is also not constrained by having to fill a certain number of pages. You can access all the articles that have ever been published in their print edition on a digital platform website.

In addition, the time for publication has been dramatically reduced. Publishers are no longer waiting for production delays. This makes it possible to publish digital media quickly after editing.

Advertisements in print media are limited for publishers. However, digital publishing platforms make advertising interactive. Multiple ads can be inserted by publishers, and consumers will be able to click on compelling CTAs (calls-to-action) that will take them to the advertiser's website.

Understanding a Publishing Company's Core Competencies

Researchers must understand the core competencies and business model of each digital publishing company. Here are a few considerations aspiring publishers should keep in mind:

- What is the researcher's intended audience?
- Does the content we publish have relevance and uniqueness?
- What are our content development strategies?

The ideal business model for publishing company is one that allows the publisher to provide high-quality, relevant content while increasing the number of readers.

> With the rise of digital publications, the
> bookshelf will soon become redundant.
> —Laura Cheng

Exposure of Research Papers to Social Media

Digital publishing platforms are boosted by social media. By sharing links from their websites or uploading their media to social media, publishers can increase their visibility. Furthermore, social media platforms like Facebook, Twitter, and Pinterest allow readers to share content, which can result in more views, organic traffic, and new subscribers.

The Dominance of Visual Content of Your research paper

By presenting readers with visual content, readers are more likely to spend more time on a website or media channel. Furthermore, it helps drive emotions to motivate audiences to act.

> A digital library will soon make
> the bookshelf obsolete.
> —Laura Cheng

Chapter 21

Tips for Choosing the Right Platform for Digital Publishing for Young Researchers

> Unless it comes with user-friendly features,
> usability will remain a white elephant.
> —Laura Cheng

How do you choose the best digital publishing platform? That's the question most young researchers and young scientists alike ask. It's easy to get overwhelmed by the hundreds of options, each with its own features and tools.

Different types of research paper require different types of digital platforms. There are some designed for general use, while others are customised for specific industries, such as medical research. Some platforms cater to self-publishing, while others require outside help. Some platforms charge a fee, whereas others are free of charge.

> A researcher must adapt to the rising trend of digital publication and remove any nostalgic feeling for traditional publication.
> —Laura Cheng

> Researchers must adapt to the growing trend of digital publication and lose their nostalgic attachment to traditional publications.
> —Laura Cheng

How do you determine which digital platform is best for your publication, and how do you go about choosing it?

Using a publishing platform that fits your needs as a researcher might be challenging. Perhaps you require an entirely self-service platform with a user-friendly interface. Possibly, you have experience working with coding languages and are comfortable working with HTML on your own.

Your digital publishing platform should support the ad software you use if you run display advertising. Whether or not you select a digital publishing platform depends greatly on the types of your publication.

You can choose the best digital publishing platform for your research paper by following these tips:

Select an open-source publication platform.

Open-source publishing platforms, such as ResearchGate and Acedemia.Edu, are free and accessible to anyone. They facilitate the publishing of research articles and remove them from their platforms. Thousands of research articles are published on those platforms every year.

Choose an interface that is intuitive.

Regardless of what digital publishing platform you choose, you'll spend hours immersed in its backend. The use of an intuitive interface will save you time and prevent resources from being wasted. If you choose a popular digital publishing platform like WordPress, you'll be able to onboard new editorial staffers without spending time on extensive training. In addition to being flexible, well-designed interfaces can be customised to meet the needs of different teams. The editorial, advertising, and marketing teams can all work closely together in the same system, reducing redundancies and ensuring that publications run more efficiently.

Try to find a platform that integrates well with others.

Most digital publishers have a Facebook page. As an alternative to Apple News, you can also use AMP for the distribution of your content. Working with these outside players can be easier or more difficult, depending on the digital publishing platform you choose. Publishers can integrate third-party services into their websites by using official or officially-endorsed plugins offered by the more-established publishing platforms. It's best to use a platform like WordPress, as it offers more third-party plugins than anyone else.

Avoid platform that uses overly-complicated software

A user-friendly publishing platform is a tool that easily publish your research content digitally. The best is what we all want. The easiest technology tends to be the most popular among publishers. You should avoid overly-complicated software and the latest technology fads. Even though there will always be newer, more modern systems, established platforms like ResearchGate and Academia.Edu have stood the test of time for a reason.

> In the absence of user-friendly features,
> usability will remain a white elephant.
> —Laura Cheng

Chapter 22

An Overview of How to Publish in a Scientific Journal

> The pace of scientific advancement
> and the spread of scientific knowledge
> is directly correlated with the number
> of research papers published.
> —Laura Cheng

Overview

Science advances when researchers do high-quality research. The authors develop unique hypotheses, rely on robust data, and use a methodologically-sound research approach. Writing up their findings, they aim to provide theoretical insight as well as to share the theoretical and practical implications of their research. Then they submit their manuscripts to peer-reviewed journals for publication. This is the most difficult part of research for many young researchers.

This chapter is designed to identify common pitfalls and provide solutions for the preparation of more impactful papers, which will be useful for doctoral students and other young researchers. These guidelines take a holistic approach to the writing of research articles, whether they are short communications or review papers, from the perspective of the management, education, information sciences, and social sciences disciplines, including a literature review.

As an academic writer, it's important to understand that rejections in academic journals can be caused by several factors. Moreover, peer-reviewing a manuscript for a journal is a necessary component of publication because no writer could anticipate and address all potential problems with a manuscript.

Guidelines for Publishing Your Research Paper

Your article should not be submitted in a hurry.

You do not have to submit your manuscript for publication once its conclusion has been crafted. When it comes to reviewing their work's shortcomings, authors sometimes rely on the assumption that they will always address them after feedback from the journal's editor and reviewers has been received.

Rejection and disappointment can be reduced with a proactive approach. It is my opinion that a logical flow of activities should be followed during every research activity as well as when preparing a manuscript. Consider rereading your manuscript at different times and possibly in different locations. The process of rereading helps identify the most common problems and deficiencies in a manuscript that might otherwise go unnoticed.

In addition, I find it very helpful to share your manuscripts with your colleagues and other researchers in your network as well as to receive their feedback. As part of this process, highlight any parts of the manuscript that need to be clarified.

Choose the appropriate publication platform.

Finding the right journal for your article can dramatically increase your chances of acceptance and ensure that it reaches your intended audience. Consult colleagues about the most appropriate journal to submit your manuscript to.

For instance, Elsevier offers a unique search facility on its website called Journal Finder. To find the most appropriate journals for their article, authors enter the article title, a brief abstract, and the field of study.

It is not uncommon for scholars who are less experienced to submit their research to more than one journal at the same time. It is recommended that authors submit one manuscript at a time to all scholarly journals to follow the research ethics and policies. If done otherwise, it can cause embarrassment and cause copyright issues with the university employer and the journals involved.

A goal journal will provide authors with guidelines as well as objectives and scopes. It is important that you know what these are.

Following several revisions of your manuscript, receiving feedback from your colleagues, and choosing an appropriate journal, the next important step is to review the aims and scope of the journals in your research area.

Taking this step may increase the chances of your manuscript being published. Another important step is to download and read the author guidelines and make sure your manuscript follows them. One out of five papers submitted to journals doesn't meet style and formatting guidelines, which may specify requirements for figures, tables, and references.

Different types of rejection can occur at different times and in different formats. As an example, if your research objective doesn't match the aims and scope of the target journal, if your manuscript isn't structured and formatted according to the target journal layout, or if the manuscript doesn't have a reasonable chance of meeting the target journal's publishing expectations, the manuscript may be rejected by the editor without being sent out for peer review.

Rejection by the desk can be disheartening for authors, who may feel that they have wasted their time or even lose motivation to continue their research.

With the title and abstract, you can make an excellent first impression.

Titles and abstracts are the first parts of a manuscript that are seen by journal editors, so they are extremely important. The following are essentials that researchers must pay attention to:

The *title* should convey your contribution to the theory and summarise the article's main theme.

A *well-written abstract* should include the aim and scope of the study, the possible solution to the problem and theory, the data set used, the key findings, the limitations, and the implications.

Your manuscript, including the main text, list of references, tables, and figures, should be copyedited by a professional editing firm, not just proofread.

Clarity is an essential attribute of scientific writing. You should hire a professional editing firm to copyedit your manuscript before submitting it for publication.

The editorial board of a peer-reviewed journal scrutinises articles before they are selected for peer review. Approximately 30–50% of articles submitted to Elsevier journals are rejected before they reach the peer-review stage, and poor language is one of the top reasons for rejection.

Writing, editing, and presenting your text properly will result in error-free and understandable text, as well as a professional image that will ensure that you can take your work seriously in the publishing industry. When a reviewer requests major revisions, they may require another edit round.

Preparing at the author's end can help facilitate the editing process. The first is to review their own manuscript for accuracy and wordiness (avoid unnecessary or normative descriptions like "it should be noted here" or "the authors believe") and only send the manuscript to an editor once it is complete in all respects and ready to be published.

It is simply not financially feasible to have professional editors edit your article multiple times. While applications such as Microsoft Word's spelling and grammar checker and Grammarly's grammar checker are certainly worthwhile, the benefits of editing your article are undeniable.

Attach a cover letter to the manuscript.

There can be no overstatement of the value of a cover letter addressed to the editor or editor in chief of the target journal. The cover letter is an important opportunity for authors to convince reviewers that their research is worthy of consideration.

Therefore, it is also necessary to spend time on the cover letter's content. Occasionally, inexperienced scholars paste the abstract from an article into the cover letter, believing that it will provide enough evidence for publication; this is a practice to avoid.

It is good practice to outline the paper's main theme in the cover letter to argue the novelty of the paper and then to argue the relevance of the manuscript to the journal in question.

A cover letter should be no longer than half a page. In the cover letter, it is important to acknowledge peers and colleagues who read and provided feedback on the article before its submission.

You should carefully consider the comments of the reviewers.

In general, editors and editors in chief frame the acceptance of a manuscript as subject to a "revise and resubmit" process based on the recommendations provided by the reviewer or reviewers.

The manuscript may require major or minor revisions brought about by these reviews. There are a few key aspects of the revision process that novice scholars should know: First, it is imperative to address all the comments received from the reviewers and avoid oversights. Second, the revised manuscript must be resubmitted by the journal's deadline. Third, the revision process may involve multiple rounds.

Two major documents are required for the revision process: First, there is the revised manuscript, which outlines all the changes made in response to the reviewers' suggestions. Second, the authors provide a response listing all the concerns of reviewers and editors they have addressed. This documentation needs to be carefully crafted.

Typically, authors are encouraged to agree with the comments of reviewers, but they are not required to follow their recommendations. They must, in all cases, provide a well-argued reason for their decision.

Summary

Because of the ever-increasing number of manuscripts submitted for publication, it can be a challenge to prepare a manuscript well enough to have it accepted by a journal.

Only a small percentage of articles are accepted by high-impact journals, although special issues and special topic sections typically have acceptance rates in the range of 40%. Often scholars must accept that their articles will be rejected and then reworked for submission to a different journal before the manuscript is accepted.

While the advice offered here is not exhaustive, it is also not difficult to follow. While these suggestions will require attention, planning, and careful implementation, following them could help doctoral students and other scholars improve their chances of getting published, which is essential for a successful, exciting, and rewarding academic career.

> The speed of advancement of science
> and the spread of scientific knowledge
> corresponds directly to the amount
> of research papers published.
> —Laura Cheng

Chapter 23

An Introduction to Research Paper Types for Undergraduates

> Good researchers are dedicated,
> diligent, and driven by a desire to
> understand the results they produce.
> —Laura Cheng

This chapter covers only the definition of research paper, analytical, comparative, interpretative, and experimental research paper.

As you progress through your academic career, you will be assigned a variety of papers. Each of these assignments has a specific purpose. Students or young scientists must first understand the types of research papers they are writing before they attempt to write one.

It is rare for professors to assign meaningless assignments. Most homework assignments are intended to demonstrate your knowledge and skills regarding a particular subject. Throughout the course, you have been required to demonstrate mastery of the material you were taught.

It is vital to adhere to the guidelines of the specific assignment that has been assigned. In doing this, you demonstrate that you are not only familiar with the material that was presented, but also that you are capable of following directions as given by the teacher.

Generally, the complexity of a research paper depends on the type of assignment, the number of sources, and the length. Typically, a research paper consists of a long essay that includes evidence that is analysed.

It is common for students in universities or colleges to be given such assignments to learn how to conduct research and analyse information. The subject does not have to conduct severe experiments about the analysis and calculation of data in this case.

Moreover, students must conduct a comprehensive search of the Internet or libraries for credible secondary sources to obtain potential answers to their questions.

This way, students gather information on topics and can take sides, present unique viewpoints, or explain new ideas. As a result, typical research papers are based on an analysis of primary and secondary sources without serious experimentation or data.

Types of Research Papers

What is a research paper?

Research papers are substantial essays that present a writer's interpretation, evaluation, or argument. The purpose of writing an essay is to use all the information and thoughts you have about a subject. The purpose of a research paper is to build on what you know about the subject matter and make a deliberate effort to learn what the experts know. As part of the research process, one surveys a field of knowledge to find the most relevant information. Creating an orderly and focused survey is possible if you know what to do.

What is an analytical research paper?

When writing an analytical paper for a course, there is a specific methodology to follow. The purpose of an analytical paper is to demonstrate to your professor not only your ability to present material objectively but also your ability to communicate this information in an informal and professional manner.

A formal analytical paper requires you to fragment a subject into sections and to analyse each one individually to summarise and draw a conclusion overall.

Generally, the author must remain objective when composing a text, but if you are requested to express your own opinion, you may also do so in a subjective manner. An analytical paper is comprised of three parts: a thesis statement, a body that proves the analysis, and a conclusion that ties everything together and concludes the paper. The method involves analysing an issue and structuring the text with a thesis statement, supporting evidence, and a conclusion.

What is a comparative research paper?

The purpose of a comparative research paper is to highlight the similarities and differences between the two subjects. There might be some similarities or exact differences between the two subjects.

College students often write this type of paper. It is, therefore, vital to learn proper writing techniques.

The objective of the comparative research is to compare the similarities and differences in a systematic manner, ensure that the subject is clearly explained to the readers, and describe the advantages and disadvantages of two things.

Furthermore, a comparative paper addresses the similarity and difference between ideas, items, events, views, concepts, etc. A comparative research paper is not limited to any topic. It can be applied to almost any subject or area with some connection.

What is an interpretative research paper?

In interpretive research paper, students are required to analyse and interpret a subject into its constituent parts and then offer a meaning or alternative meanings for each of the components.

To write an interpretive research paper requires critical analysis. Almost all students will be required to write an interpretive analysis essay in their introductory literature courses as well as in their intermediate and advanced literature courses.

The interpretive research paper describes an analysis of another piece of writing. An interpretive essay assignment may seem daunting. It is not impossible to determine where to begin, which literary elements to analyse, and which concepts to interpret.

What is an experimental research paper?

Experimental research is a study that conforms to a scientific research design. A hypothesis is accompanied by a variable that can be controlled by the researcher, as well as variables that can be measured, calculated, and compared.

Experiments are conducted under controlled conditions. Researchers collect data, and the results will either support or refute the hypothesis. An example of this method of research is hypothesis testing or deductive research

Research papers of this type describe in detail a particular experiment. These papers are commonly found in the sciences, such as physics, chemistry, and biology. The goal of an experiment is to explain a certain outcome or phenomenon with a certain set of actions. You should provide supporting data for your experiment and analyse it adequately.

> An excellent researcher should see
> what no one else has seen and think
> what no one else has thought.
> —Laura Cheng

Chapter 24

A Brief Guide for Writing Analytical Research Papers

> The same as a ship needs a compass for navigation in the ocean, writing any research paper requires a guide to help you navigate through the writing process.
> —Laura Cheng

Guidelines are only meant to serve as a guide. It may be necessary to modify the guidelines so that they are more relevant to the research articles of young researchers.

Creating the Framework

There is a specific framework for every research paper. Similar to other tasks, your analytical research paper will follow a similar format, but the purpose here is much more specific. Any topic should be dissected and broken down into different segments for analysis. There will not be a regular comparison and contrast approach.

An analysis paper's introduction is one of its most important components. The thesis statement is presented here. This statement serves as the direction for your entire analytical process as well as indicating what your essay is about. It also indicates what you will be presenting as well as the argument you will be presenting. The validity of the work, as well as the purpose of writing it, will be unclear if you fail to make the thesis statement clear.

How to write the abstract and the introduction of an analytical paper?

The abstract and introduction of an analytical paper serve to engage the reader and persuade them to continue reading. Here are some guidelines to assist you in composing an introduction:

- Describe what you intend to accomplish. Be as engaging and interesting as possible to persuade the reader that it is worth reading.
- Describe the topic of the paper concisely. Don't include too many facts as those will be contained in the body of the text.
- Keep the text brief, clear, and concise. Make them want to read more and find the answers they are looking for by engaging them, attracting them, and attracting their interest. The answer you provide will either prove that you are knowledgeable about the subject or that you need to revise further.

Remember that search engines and bibliographic databases use the abstract and title to identify key terms for indexing your published papers. For this reason, the abstract and title of your paper or article are crucial to help other researchers find it.

Body Section of Your Paper

This is the part of the paper where you will present the information to the reader.

Here comes your proof—the explanation of your thesis statement. In this section of the paper, you will dissect the entire topic and break it down into sections for analysis. It is important to present your point first, to support it with evidence, and then to conclude your essay.

In the body of the analytical paper, you will most likely cite at least two or three arguments that support your thesis and provide cohesive evidence and responses to base it on.

The Conclusion of the Analytical Paper

In conclusion, you reaffirm all the points that you have made throughout the paper and then bring them together cohesively into one valid conclusion.

To accomplish this, it is best to restate the thesis statement, then further elaborate on the main points, tying them together, and conclude with the holistic nature of your argument. The conclusion is merely a summary of what you have presented in the body of your paper, as well as a statement of the thesis. It is not a place to add additional evidence or introduce additional points not discussed in the body.

To be poignant here is of utmost importance. You are only required to analyse whatever subject you choose. Therefore, it is important that you outline and make clear what you are trying to convey to your reader when choosing your thesis statement. The conclusion is of equal importance to the introduction in that it sets the tone and establishes the outline of the paper. Consequently, they form a symbiotic relationship to create a solid and reliable paper.

Summary of this Chapter

An analytical paper involves analysing a topic, segmenting it to analyse the thesis statement, and concluding the essay by tying together the points made in the body of the paper. The thesis statement and conclusion form the cornerstones of the paper, the cornerstone of the essay. While the entire paper is important, establishing your stance and establishing your thesis will determine the validity of your paper. You are attempting to convince the reader that you have an understanding and command of the topic you have chosen.

Chapter 25

A Brief Guide for Writing Interpretation Research Paper

> To feel at home in the world of
> research, one must establish roots
> and become integrated with it.
> —Laura Cheng

An analysis essay focuses on analysing a literary piece and discovering the most interesting aspects of that work. The most effective method of beginning is to select a scene, character, activity, line, or some other part of a literary work, then separate this part into smaller parts, and analyse each part individually.

It is best to analyse these segments of the work by using the elements of literature to explain their meanings, compare each segment with other sections of the work, or apply a literary theory to each segment.

Ensure that your analysis is logical. It is also important to ensure that the structure of the essay is balanced and contains a brief introduction, several well-organised body paragraphs that focus on one point, and a brief conclusion. The introduction may also be followed by a summary of the main points of the work in the first body section.

What should be included in the interpretive analysis essay?

There should be an introduction, a body, and a conclusion in an interpretative analysis essay.

It is imperative that the writer consistently quotes and paraphrases the literary work throughout the introduction, body, and conclusion to assist in their analysis and to determine the meaning of the text.

Using quotations and paraphrases to support their arguments allows the writer to clearly show what the author has written and to anticipate their own interpretation of the quoted text.

The writer as well should quote, paraphrase, and reference other literary works and professional critics. By including additional quotations, the writer can develop a well-supported interpretation of the work they are analysing. Finally, all citations and bibliographies must be formatted according to APA, MLA, or the style specified by the lecturer.

Tips for Composing an Interpretive Essay

It is imperative that you come up with a new, interesting, or unique approach to interpreting the literacy work.

There is the option of either concentrating on the larger meaning of the whole work or concentrating on some specific meaning in a particular aspect of the work, such as traits, symbols, and settings.

It is important that you provide a variety of reasons why you believe that your interpretation is correct. Furthermore, assume the audience has already read the literary work.

It is very important that you provide each reason with a quote or paraphrase from the source.

The final draft of the paper should contain the introduction and the conclusion, which summarise the entire work.

> A researcher can only feel at home in
> the research world once he establishes
> roots and integrates into it.
> —Laura Cheng

Chapter 26

How to Write a Comparative Analysis Paper

> Comparison of research results is essential
> for the advancement of science.
> —Laura Cheng

Researchers are required to write papers comparing two things throughout your academic career: two experimental results, two different theories, two scientific processes, etc.

Often researchers are required to compare two experimental results regardless of the similarities or differences between them, for example, two pesticides with totally different effects on the environment or two similar things with completely different perspectives but having surprising similarities.

When faced with a list of seemingly-unrelated similarities and differences, you may wonder how to make a paper that is more than just a mechanical exercise in which you state all the features A and B share and then all the ways in which A and B differ. A paper of this type usually asserts A and B are similar but not so much after all. You must take your raw data, the similarities and differences you've observed, and weave them into a coherent argument.

General Guidelines for Writing a Comparative Paper

Defining the Context or Framework

Comparing and contrasting two things requires a context, a framework. It is the umbrella under which you have grouped them. Generally, a frame of reference consists of an idea, a theme, a question, a problem, or a theory; a group of similar items from which you extract two for attention; biographical or historical details.

Reference frames are best derived from specific sources rather than your own observations. In a paper where you compare how two writers define masculinity, you would do better to cite a sociologist's views than to spin out potentially-uninteresting theories of your own.

Most assignments specify exactly what the frame of reference should be, and most courses give you sources for developing it. You must provide your own frame of reference if an assignment does not provide one. There would be no context for a paper without any angle on the subject, no frame or focus for a meaningful argument to be presented.

The Basis for Comparison

Imagine you are writing a paper on global food distribution, and you compare apples and oranges. Why those two? Why not pears or bananas? Give your reader a sense of why your choice was deliberate, not random, by providing the rationale behind your choice. For example, in a paper asking how domesticity is related to abortion, the comparison is obvious; the issue has two opposing sides: pro-choice and pro-life. Choosing two forest sites for comparing acid rain effects is less obvious. If comparing a new forest stand in the White Mountains with an old forest in the same region, the paper will be set up differently than one focusing on similar-aged forests in Maine and the Catskills. The reasoning behind your choice must be explained.

Comparative Thesis

Your comparisons anticipate the comparative nature of your thesis. Any argumentative paper must have a thesis that conveys the gist of your argument, which necessarily follows from your frame of reference. Comparing two things depends on how they are related, but the thesis relates to how you choose the two things to compare. Are they corroborated, contradicted, corrected, or debated? When writing a compare-and-contrast paper, you can indicate the precise relationship between A and B by using the word "whereas" or the similarity between A and B; you must make the relationship clear. Any paper that compares two things is very dependent on this relationship.

Organising Structure

You should describe your context, grounds for comparison, and thesis in your introduction. The body of your paper may be organised in two basic ways: text by text or point by point.

During text-by-text discussion, you discuss all of A, followed by all of B. In a point-by-point approach, you alternate points about A with comparable points about B.

Using a text-by-text scheme if you believe B extends A; using a point-by-point scheme if A and B are engaged in debate.

The point-by-point scheme can, however, seem like ping-pong. By grouping multiple points together, you can reduce the number of times you alternate between A and B. No matter what organisational scheme you choose, similarities and differences must not be equal.

The more quickly you get to your argument, the more interesting your paper will be. So a paper comparing two evolutionary theorists' interpretations of specific archaeological findings might only have two or three sentences in the introduction on similarities and perhaps only a paragraph or two to set up the contrast. Text by text or point by point, the remainder of the paper will treat the differences between the two theorists.

Connecting A and B

Every point in an argumentative paper must be connected to the thesis. Linking new sections will allow your reader to see the logical and systematic progression of the argument. When writing a compare-and-contrast essay, you'll also need to make connections between A and B.

> Researchers of the highest level should see what no one else has seen and think what no one else has thought.
> —Laura Cheng

Chapter 27

Guidelines for Writing Research Report

> Researchers talk with their pens in addition to carrying out good experiments.
> —Laura Cheng

In terms of the variety and complexity of writing tasks, the task of writing a report is one of the most challenging. There is no doubt that writing a report, whether it is for academic use or for business purposes, is an extremely-powerful means of providing new information, data, investigations, research, data analysis, and other types of information to those who want to use that information. The term "report" is defined as an orderly and systematic presentation of information that provides support for the problem-solving and decision-making process.

Clearly presenting the analysis and statistics of the factors relevant to a specific matter is one of the most important purposes of a report as it serves as an investigative and decision-making tool. In addition to its use in planning and evaluating initiatives, such a research paper can also provide important analytical information regarding key resources and other important aspects of a project.

Various types of reports exist, each with a unique structure and format; however, this chapter focuses on academic reports.

In most fields of study, students are often required to write research reports as part of their assessment, especially in the sciences and engineering. The purpose of drafting a research report is to provide a clear understanding of the subject of your research, the analysis performed during the study, and the results that you obtained.

How to write a good research report?

An important feature of a good research report is the presence of the following: accuracy of the information, high degree of precision and objectivity, aspects of relevance, providing clarity, and formatted perfectly.

Accuracy of Information

It is important for a researcher of a report to be careful when quoting facts and figures. Because the information given in the report is based on research, the findings and analysis are used to reach crucial decisions; a researcher must gather information from academic and legitimate sources, and he/she must proofread the information at least twice to avoid presenting incorrect data.

The High Degree of Precision and Objectivity

Any aspiring scientist, before initiating the process of writing a report on any academic topic, should know that such a research paper should be objective in nature, i.e., should not be influenced by the author's opinion. As part of the professional essay writing process, a writer is also definite about the purpose of the report from the outset and sticks to it throughout the process. When a report is written with precision, it can be turned into a valuable research paper because it will bring credibility and trust to the conclusions or information that are presented in it.

Aspects of Relevance

The relevance of a report is another characteristic of a high-quality report. It is very important that a report writer should include all empirical evidence, statistics, and facts related to the actual topic or objective of the report. A paper can be weakened and its conclusions unreliable if it cites information from irrelevant sources. The key to finding useful information here is not to look for everything from scholarly sources but to provide proper reference notes and to only look for relevant pieces of information from scholarly sources, such as journals, published reports, books, etc. The success of a research report depends largely on the accuracy of the date and the relevance of the facts contained in the report.

Providing Clarity

As part of the academic report, a student must prepare a rough outline of the points that will be included in the document. The use of pointers will help ensure that all the main points of the report are addressed. It is essential to also ensure that the language of the report is as clear and concise as possible. Whenever possible, try avoiding long sentences and complicated terms. However, the language must be formal and academic at the same time.

Perfectly Formatted

It is important that your report follows a standard format that includes a title page, abstract, introduction, research or analysis, results/findings, and conclusion.

Chapter 28

How to Structure a Research Paper?

> A good research paper answers
> a specific research question and
> challenges the reader's perspective.
> —Laura Cheng

Not everybody is good at writing well-structured research papers. Some research papers take months or years to complete. Writing might seem impossible at times. Then there is the structure of the research paper.

A good structured research paper can answer a specific research question. A great research paper will challenge the reader's perspective.

The structure of a research paper is determined by the requirements of the assignment. There are times when students receive their assignments and instructions, and they need to analyse specific research questions or topics, find appropriate sources, and write final papers.

When a manuscript is well-formatted, authors are better able to present their views, analyses, and research results in a scientific manner. There is consistency in the research paper, and as a result, the reader can concentrate on the content.

General Structure

The general structure of a research paper consists of the following: title, abstract, outline, introduction, literature review, methodology, results, discussion, recommendations, limitations, conclusion, acknowledgements, and references.

Some of these sections might not be included by students because of the different types of research papers that they are assigned and because of the specific instructions that they have. For example, if the instructions of the papers do not assume that real experiments will be conducted, the methodology section may be skipped since there are no data to back it up.

Cited below is the example of a typical structure of a final research paper.

Title

The title page of your journal article is the first thing the reader sees; it helps them understand the subject and scope of your research paper. There should be enough information on the title page about the primary authors of the research paper and whether the research has been reviewed and tested for use as a study design. Credentials of the author are particularly important when it comes to evaluating the credibility of research papers. Additionally, you may also include information about the organisation that provided financial aid and support for your research or any other agency that supported your research.

Abstract

A research abstract refers to the first paragraph of a research paper that gives a brief description of the purpose of the study, research questions or suggestions, and main findings and conclusions.

It is recommended that this paragraph of about 150–200 words be written when the whole project has already been finished. Therefore, abstract sections should include a description of the main findings of the studies, along with a discussion of their relevance.

Introduction

The introduction describes briefly what the problem statements are, what the methods of analysis are, what the key findings are, and what the conclusion is. There are many aspects of a research paper that form this section. Basically, it contains the rationale for the work or background research, an explanation and defence of the importance, a brief description of the experimental design, the defined research questions, hypotheses, or important features.

Literature Review

It is important to conduct a literature review to gain understanding of the research questions or topics through analysis of past studies or scholarly articles. Therefore, the aim of this section is to summarise and synthesise arguments and ideas from scholarly sources without adding a new perspective. This part then has been organised according to arguments and ideas rather than specific sources.

Methodology of the Study

It discusses the design of the research as well as explains the rationale for the design. As a rule, it is necessary to describe techniques for gathering information and other aspects related to experiments in a research report. Students and scholars, for example, should describe the specialised materials that have been used and the general procedure. Depending on how the study is judged scientifically, individuals may use some or all the methods in future studies or judge the scientific merit of the study. Scientists should also explain in detail the way they plan to carry out their experiments.

Results

After research or experiment, the results are the information that has been gained or the data that has been collected. Generally, findings should be presented and illustrated. In addition, this section might contain tables or figures.

Analysis of the Results

The analysis of the results of the study is called a discussion, which happens in a separate section within the research paper. The purpose of the discussion is to evaluate the findings of the study or to compare it with past studies. Specifically, the purpose is to interpret gained data or findings in an appropriate and thoughtful manner. If, for instance, the results do not match the expectations at the beginning of the experiment, scientists should explain why it may have occurred. However, when results confirm the rationale, scientists should describe the theories that are supported by the evidence.

Recommendation

A recommendation comes from a discussion where scholars propose new ideas and potential solutions based on the results they obtained from the research paper. If scientists have any recommendations on how to improve this research, to make it better for other scholars to use in further studies, they must write what they think in this section.

Limitations

It is important to consider research weaknesses and results to be able to get new directions when addressing limitations. As an example, if a researcher finds any limitations of a particular study that could have an impact on experiments, this knowledge must not be used by scholars because the same errors have been made in the past. Additionally, scientists should avoid contradictory results, and even more so, they should cite them in this section.

Conclusions of a Conducted Research

The conclusions of a research paper are based on the results of the research. There are basically two parts to this section, one covering the final thoughts and the other summing up everything. It should also be noted that this part can be used in place of limitations and recommendations that are too small on their own. In this case, scientists do not have to use headings to identify recommendations and limitations.

Acknowledgement

An acknowledgement or an appendix can take many forms, ranging from paragraphs to charts to tables. Here, scholars provide additional information on the research paper they are writing.

References

Referencing is the process by which students, scholars, or scientists provide a list of all the sources they used and how they obtained them by following the format and rules of academic writing.

Chapter 29

Mistakes Young Researchers Make When Writing Literature Reviews

> The publication is the crowning achievement of research, so avoid making any mistakes.
> —Laura Cheng

Why must you avoid making mistakes?

It is the publication of a research paper that is the crowning achievement of the process. It represents the culmination of the process of the research.

What is a literature review?

It is important to understand what a literature review is and why you need to write one before knowing the common mistakes.

A literature review is considered crucial as it forms the basis for your dissertation or thesis. The description, summary, and evaluation of the previous research should be brief and clear. It provides a theoretical foundation for your research. Identifying a research gap is the primary goal of a literature review.

Literature reviews are comprehensive summaries of the research that has already been done on a given topic in the past. The literature review assists the author and the reader to gain a clear understanding of what has happened or what has been established in the past in terms of their research area.

Accordingly, it informs the readers that the author has considered the bulk of the major work done by many researchers in the field.

There are two general types of literature reviews: as a component of a full academic paper or article (literature review-based paper) or as a section of a teaching essay, article, or dissertation.

In this chapter, we will discuss some of the common mistakes that academic writers make when performing an academic literature review when writing a research paper, a dissertation, or a thesis. The information presented here will help you improve your writing skills.

Using Emotional Phrases

It is recommended not to use emotional phrases in a literature review section because of the danger of over-emotionalising the topic. It is important to keep in mind that the writing of a literature review requires you to present the flow of ideas regarding your research area.

Giving Personal Opinions

Do not use emotional phrases. It is highly recommended that you refrain from inserting personal views in your review writing. In such a review, ideas and research relating to the topic are presented in an unbiased way.

Being Overly-Descriptive

There are many aspects of the literature review that must go beyond just summarising what has already been published by other researchers. It should also look for any shortcomings or limitations in their methodology. Describe why you might doubt the validity of their conclusions, for example, given the small size of the sample or vague measurements that were taken. This kind of feedback is desired by all tutors.

Insufficient Quality of Sources

It is expected that per 1,000 words, at least ten scholarly references will be cited. There should be most peer-reviewed articles, with occasional theoretical books and research reports, published within the last three years. To conduct a literature review, it is not appropriate to use books, magazines, newspapers, or blogs as sources.

Structure-Based Articles

It is always a temptation to talk about one article in one paragraph and then move on to the next. This is the simplest way to write a literature review! Do not succumb to this temptation. Aside from descriptiveness, the structure-based article is what most tutors strongly dislike, along with descriptiveness. In each paragraph, you should compare the findings from three or more articles.

Not Linking the Research Question

There are several scholarly sources that can be used and analysed in a critical manner, but this is not sufficient. Explain how these findings help you answer your research question and what you can learn from them about your topic.

Unfounded Statements

It is very easy to become judgmental when criticising the work of others. Whenever you make a statement, make sure to back it up with a reference to another source so your readers will understand that you're not just expressing your own opinion.

> Research ends in publication,
> so avoid mistakes.
> —Laura Cheng

Chapter 30

Literature Review Issues and Solutions

Insufficient Background/Definition Section

This occurs more often, and unfortunately, most tertiary students don't focus on putting the pre-literature review section at the end. Including one is very important since it provides information on the background of the research. When key concepts and background information are not included in a presentation, a substantial portion of the potential audience is left out.

Poorly-Organised and Structured Literature Review

The most common mistake in literature review writing is a bad organisational structure that forces the student to rewrite and restructure sections of the review. It is possible to avoid the poor structure of a literature review by using subheadings.

If such a method is employed in the review, the focus remains on the bigger picture to eliminate illogical structure and poor organisation.

Inappropriate Content

A doctoral student is most likely to become engrossed in the details of the review, particularly when reading other studies. As a result, they may write or mention irrelevant topics. Cite only relevant points related to your subheadings to ensure that the literature review contains the relevant information. Even if a study is essential to a topic, it does not mean all the details are pertinent.

Study Types

While writing a literature review, the most common mistake authors make is to include only old papers or to include papers that have just been published. In fact, authors should try to include old and recent studies in the review.

There is no literature gap.

The main purpose of doing a literature review is to identify a gap in the literature. If your literature review is incapable of highlighting a research gap or a contribution to the field, then your study will not be of any value.

> You will never achieve perfection if you fear it.
> —Laura Cheng

Chapter 31

Common Mistakes in Scientific Writing

> It is wise to learn from our mistakes,
> but to learn from other individuals'
> mistakes is truly brilliant.
> —Laura Cheng

The process of writing a scientific manuscript requires a lot of practice, and we tend to make the same mistakes repeatedly. This chapter summarises the most common errors, as well as how to avoid them, to help you improve your writing.

I realised that we all tend to make similar mistakes after reviewing several papers on communication, science, and writing a few manuscripts myself. The errors made by our students are often the same.

Common mistakes should be avoided when writing a manuscript.

Not-Thoroughly-Reviewed Background Literature

Make sure that before you even begin designing your study, you have read all relevant papers and that you are up to date with all relevant research papers. To support your findings and to argue why your study is important, which knowledge gap it is closing, or to justify your conclusions, it is important to present the complete background of your study in the introduction. Please remember that the papers' reviewers are most likely to be fellow researchers who are very familiar with the research topic and will notice if important sections of earlier research have been omitted.

Unclear Research Objectives, Hypotheses, and Predictions

In your introduction, you should state clearly what your research objectives, hypotheses, and predictions are—all based on a literature review you presented, in which you highlighted what remains unknown. It will not be possible for the reader to follow the paper if they cannot understand why your study was conducted.

Confusing Structure of the Manuscript

Your reader may not be able to follow the sequence of your hypotheses, methods, results, and discussion. For that reason, it is important to maintain a consistent order throughout the manuscript.

An example would be if you have mentioned hypothesis A, B, and C, you keep that order in the methods section as well as the results and discussion.

First, you should describe how you tested hypothesis A (methods), what were the results of testing hypothesis A (results) and how do the results support hypothesis A, and how does it relate to other studies (discussion). Then you do the same thing with your other hypothesis.

In every part of the manuscript, you should briefly reference your hypothesis before explaining the methods, results, or discussing it to facilitate the reader's understanding. By doing this, you will also be more likely to keep a good flow and structure.

Insufficiently-Described Methods

In the methods section, you should describe every step you took during your study in sufficient detail so that each person can reproduce your study exactly. You should describe everything you did as well as everything you used for your research—the equipment you used, the participants and raw materials involved, timeframes, data collection, and data analysis. Detailed descriptions are necessary here.

Jumbled-Up Sections

The results should not be mixed with the discussion. Do not interpret or discuss the results when you present them in the results section, and only summarise the results briefly before discussing them. It is important that you check the authors' guidelines before you write your paper in case the journal combines results and discussion so that you do not break this rule.

Discrepancy between Conclusions Drawn and Data Presented

Statistically, the results are either significant or not. Do not state that there is a "tendency" if there are no significant results since the data does not support this notion. As a rule, you should mention those results which are close to being significant, and suggest that perhaps with larger sample size, the results would have been significant. Ensure that you support the conclusions drawn from the data in the discussion as well. The data should not be interpreted too much to fit the hypothesis.

Inaccurate Writing

Scientific writing must be accurate. Even though in appeal writing it is not recommended to use the same word twice, this does not apply to scientific writing, which must be precise.

Check your text for fill words and make sure you only use words that are necessary for understanding your sentence. Your reader will not be impressed by exotic terms or complex sentence structures.

To avoid the use of unspecific terms, such as high temperature or high humidity, use more quantitative descriptions, such as more than 35ºC or relative humidity of more than 85%.

Make it a habit to always use the active voice, as it is more concise and clearer than using the passive voice.

Incomplete References and/or Citations

In your manuscript, you should make sure to credit all the studies whose results you mention. Be sure to keep track of all your references.

There may be times when you give only the author and year of a citation in your text; most of the time you will give all the reference information in the reference list (author, year, title, journal, pages, DOI).

It takes a lot of time to collect them all at once, and maybe you will even have to search for the complete reference after you have finished your paper to do so. You must follow the style you have to present the citations and references required by the journal you plan to publish your manuscript in, so ensure that you are aware of the style format beforehand to avoid unnecessary work.

> Learning from our mistakes is wise, but to
> learn from others' mistakes is truly brilliant.
> —Laura Cheng

Chapter 32

An Overview of Manuscript Language

> "Book" can be noun or verb in English: My *book* is on the shelf. I *booked* the ticket.
> —Laura Cheng

What is the significance of language?

It is possible to delay or prevent publication because of poor language quality. A manuscript's presentation, particularly the language used to convey results, should be taken seriously.

A clear writing style reflects a clear mind. Scientists are concerned with more than merely recording facts. It is through written communication that knowledge is transmitted and an impact is made. In the absence of clear and proper language, readers may not grasp the full message or impact of the work.

It does not matter how cutting-edge the findings you present in your paper are. Unfortunately, poor language quality, such as misspellings and errors in grammar, could delay publication or even result in your paper being rejected.

The English language should always be used properly. Throughout the entire manuscript, ensure that proper English is used, and make sure that captions and headings are included in the figures, charts, graphs, and photographs.

Are publishers responsible for correcting linguistic errors?

It is the writer's responsibility, and resources are available. It is common for authors to assume that a publisher will correct the language of their manuscript after it has been accepted, but this assumption is incorrect.

In fact, it is the author's responsibility to ensure that a paper is in the best possible condition. As a result, it is imperative to improve the rudimentary issues related to grammar and spelling, as well as provide readers with a clear, logical, and compelling narrative.

Even though publishers do not edit language, they often provide resources to authors unfamiliar with international journal conventions.

Prior to peer review, some publishers may also perform technical screening. Your paper may be returned to you if it does not meet a journal's minimum language standards.

Manuscript Language Rules

A manuscript should be written in the following manner: accurate, concise, with clear objective.

Use a spell-checker to prevent spelling errors.

Common language errors include elements of style for writing scientific papers, grammar, sentences, paragraphs, etc.

Do not use abbreviations or acronyms and contractions. Abbreviations or acronyms should be avoided unless they are very well-known. Do not use contractions, such as *it's*, *isn't*, or *weren't*.

Citations should not be replaced by acronyms.

Abstracts and conclusions should be free of acronyms.

Remove redundant words and phrases.

Sentences are written in the manuscript language.

The first step toward writing a successful manuscript is to be aware of your sentence structure.

Keep your sentences concise and direct.

In scientific writing, sentences are typically between 12 and 18 words in length.

Do not include more than one piece of information per sentence.

Short factual sentences should be constructed.

Complex and long sentences can be confusing to the reader.

Try to avoid using more than one statement in a sentence.

Do not convey more than one idea per sentence.

Provide a clear storyline by linking sentences within a paragraph.

Related words should be kept together.

Put the subject and verb near to enable the reader to understand what the subject is doing.

Consider the order in which you write a sentence.

Within a sentence, the "stress position" provides new information to be highlighted.

There is "old" information that leads up to the point of emphasis within the "topical position." It is the topical position that comes before the stress position.

The manuscript is written in paragraph form.

Each topic should be represented by a separate paragraph. Whenever possible, start a paragraph with a topic sentence and end it in conformity with that sentence. Do not use lose sentences in succession.

Parallelism makes it easier for the reader to follow the content. Each paragraph should have a consistent tense within it.

As you are transitioning from one paragraph to another, make sure that you do so with a logical flow so the reader is guided from one topic to another. An effective paragraph is constructed in the same way as a sentence, bringing the reader from the familiar at the beginning to new ideas at the end.

How to avoid common errors?

Do not use the word *this* without qualification.

As an alternative, write, "What do you mean by 'this'?" A reader could make an incorrect guess if he must guess. Although the meaning of the words *this, that, these,* or *those* is intuitive, the author serves the reader well by clearly defining the terms.

Prepositional phrases should not be repeated too often. There is something awkward about reading prepositional phrases that run on indefinitely. Readers may quickly become fatigued by these phrases.

Ensure that the paper does not contain words or phrases that are subjective or redundant.

Adjectives that are subjective or judgmental should be avoided.

Neither the readers nor the authors should be expected to read each other's minds.

Avoid expressing beliefs in your writing. "It is our belief that this model result is accurate." Instead write, "Based on our analysis, we demonstrate that this model's outcome is consistent with the empirical data."

The communication of science is not about expressing beliefs. In fact, it involves logically identifying lines of evidence that lead to a hypothesis, theory, or conclusion based on that evidence.

Avoid vague statements and adverbs that follow each other, such as "The test results were obtained quickly and cheaply." What equipment was used to obtain the test results? How fast is "quickly"? And what is considered "cheaply" as compared to other test methods?

Chapter 33

Mistakes to Avoid in Research

> The greatest lessons in life tend to be
> learned from the worst mistakes.
> —Laura Cheng

Experiments tend to go awry, but careful planning and attention to detail can prevent accidents, loss of resources, and reputational damage.

The possibility of making a mistake at any stage of experimental research should always be considered, but it should not discourage researchers. All these mistakes can be avoided if researchers are properly trained and remain vigilant. We do better science by reducing errors as we create a safer, more productive working environment.

As the adage goes, we learn from our mistakes. In addition, most mistakes are made during the formative years of research scientists, when they are still being mentored.

Blind Reliance on Protocol

Errors can occur at various levels, and they sometimes result from blind reliance on methods that are less than optimal, whether they are common or specialised. Experimental procedures should consist of a well-thought-out protocol.

Permutations of the steps should be included in the protocol to determine the most appropriate methodological approach if the protocol is investigator-initiated.

There is no guarantee that a peer-reviewed protocol will work for all individuals. Assuming the protocol will function flawlessly the first time you apply it is a mistake.

It is also important to consider the possibility that a published protocol may have omitted important caveats, e.g., the method does not work properly when cells are in their S phase of growth. This can lead to experiments failing or resulting in inconsistent results.

It is also a mistake to disregard troubleshooting by not at least seeking advice from others who have used the method successfully in the past. The risk of a failed protocol can be reduced by getting in touch with the investigator who published the protocol.

Negligence over the Quality of Reagents

An additional research blunder involves failing to pay attention to all the reagents used in an experiment. You must check the expiration date of a given material before using it in an experiment. Reputable manufacturers conduct quality control studies to determine their products' shelf lives.

An additional mistake is the use of reagents that have not been properly stored, for example, refrigerated instead of frozen. Reagents that are perishable are particularly susceptible to this error.

No Proper Documentation of the Experiment

Documentation of experiments is another research mistake that is completely avoidable. For a successful experiment to be reproduced consistently, the laboratory notebook must contain detailed information. Each step should be documented. Materials used, variations in methods used, anything that occurred during the experiment that was not typical, e.g., a brief power outage, should all be considered. A seemingly-simple factor, such as the type of water used, can have a significant impact on an experiment. It is a mistake to ignore the "consistency imperative." For example, if your experiments call for the use of distilled water, always use distilled water instead of deionized water. Consistency is important!

Shortcuts

You should avoid taking shortcuts. In the case of an incubation of 40 minutes, be patient and wait until the entire period has elapsed before continuing. Know your time commitment when planning an experiment.

Poor Maintenance of Laboratory Equipment

Another error that can plague even the most experienced researcher is the failure to properly maintain equipment. A regular maintenance program is essential, especially when the equipment is designed to protect users from environmental hazards, e.g., fume hoods. Does the equipment have an up-to-date certification?

Failure to Observe the Manufacturer's Recommended Calibration

Another equipment-related mistake is failing to perform the manufacturer's recommended calibration. Failure to calibrate micropipettes used for measuring minute quantities of reagents is one of my pet peeves. When a protocol instructs the use of one microliter of reagent, and the micropipette used to aliquot that volume is not appropriately calibrated, significant variations in the amount of reagent used can occur, resulting in significant differences in the results of experiments.

Failure to Adhere to Laboratory Practices

A series of related mistakes that occur in laboratory settings are caused by a failure to adhere to good laboratory practices. Though we try to adhere to and advocate for these practices, we sometimes fail to comply with what our laboratory safety officers tell us to do for our own good. That is a grave error, one we cannot afford to make, if we are to ensure our own and others' safety.

> Our ability to correct our mistakes
> defines who we are.
> —Laura Cheng

Chapter 34

Common Mistakes Made by Young Researchers in Laboratory

> Avoid negative consequences by doing
> things correctly the first time.
> —Laura Cheng

Laboratory work requires concentration and hard work. In this chapter, we will discuss some of the most common errors that young researchers make while working in the laboratory.

Lab Coat

Ignoring the wearing of a lab coat in the lab or forgetting to remove it when you leave the lab—a lab coat serves the purpose of keeping nasty stuff from getting on our clothes, so it is likely that our lab coats contain nasty substances. Taking your lab coat to the office or coffee room is a bad idea, as you will transfer the nasty stuff there as well.

Material Safety Data Sheet (MSDS)

Failure to read the MSDS. You should never use a chemical without reviewing its MSDS to ensure safety. MSDS may seem as neurotic as a mother's overprotective nature, but it is easy to become blasé about safety.

Even the most overprotective and neurotic mother occasionally speaks some sense. For instance, if you recognise the potential for the formation of nitrosamines, a carcinogen, you will avoid combining amines with nitrite in corrosion chemicals.

Safety Glasses/Goggles Not Worn

No argument here. A glass/acid/powder of some sort will get into your eyes during your career. Your chances of avoiding injury may increase if you are not wearing safety glasses.

Safety specs and goggles do not provide UV protection.

UV transilluminators are known to cause serious damage if not properly protected. Isn't it amazing how many people seem to think that their standard googles protect them from ultraviolet rays? The sight of sunburned retinas is never pleasant.

Placing Your Head in the Fume Hood

Fume hoods can only protect you, and laminar flow hoods can only protect the items you are working with, if you keep your head out of the hood.

Opening Toxic or Carcinogenic Chemicals Outside of the Fume Hood

It is not recommended to open toxic or carcinogenic chemicals, such as hydrofluoric acid or formaldehyde, outside of the fume hood. Always open it the fume hood.

Making Use of the Lab as a Kitchen

Never bring food or drink into the laboratory, and do not eat, drink, or smoke in the laboratory.

Do not smell or taste any chemicals or other lab samples under any circumstances.

Working in the Lab Alone When Emotionally Exhausted

Working alone or unsupervised is never a good idea. Don't work when you are emotionally or physically exhausted.

Unattended Laboratory Experiments

In the laboratory, experiments should never be left unattended.

Never Pipette by Mouth

Pipetting should never be done by mouth because this may result in your unintentionally ingesting unwelcome chemicals.

Hands Don't Get Washed

Finally, always remember to wash your hands as your mother taught you when you were a kid, especially after handling biohazards or chemical reagents. Do this before you leave the lab.

Chapter 35

The Essentials of the Development of Writing Skills

> Society is greatly influenced by what people write and what people read.
> —Laura Cheng

> The things people write and read greatly influence our society.
> —Laura Cheng

The ability to write well, having excellent writing skills, can make you an important member of your team or company. It is also one of the most effective strategies to remain consistently employable, regardless of your profession.

It is especially alarming when you consider that employees spend up to a third of their time reading and writing e-mails according to a study conducted by Carleton University.

In addition to this, depending on the role you have, you might also have to write reports, memos, proposals, etc.

How to improve your writing skills?

It is very easy to just shoot off documents without really thinking about what needs to be done, especially when one is pressed for time, attending meetings, and having a packed schedule. However, in a world of canned messages and auto-responders, it is truly thoughtful writing that will set you apart.

It is essential that you focus on your audience as one of the requirements. Consider the needs of your readers for a few minutes, and you will end up with a more effective article.

As a rule of thumb, you could start by asking yourself the following questions:

- Who exactly is this audience?
- What is their level of knowledge about the subject/issues you are writing about?
- To what extent do they view what you write as important?
- Are there any key points that they will be looking for first?
- In your opinion, what is most important to include?
- Which types of data or supporting evidence is most valuable to them?
- If someone reads your document, what do you hope they will do, say, feel, and think about it?

The power of these questions should not be underestimated. For example, my dad once had the pleasure of working with an engineering consultant who wrote regular reports for their clients in Northern China but didn't seem to get much feedback. It was impossible for them to tell if they were doing a good job or whether their clients were happy.

They had a problem in that they wrote reports for people who were not fluent in English, some of whom did not speak English well, and they used academic jargon that was difficult to follow.

With a focus on their readers' needs, they realised that they needed to have a very different writing style to communicate effectively.

In addition, do not be afraid to directly ask people what they think about your written materials. The answers may surprise you.

> The power of questions should
> not be underestimated.
> —Laura Cheng

Do away with the frills.

It is very important to keep your writing simple at work. Use simple sentence structure, avoid flowery phrases, and do not use too much insider jargon. Usually, people tend to overestimate the level of knowledge that their readers possess about topics that they already have a lot of experience with. You still will not get extra points for making the readers work hard to understand what you have written, even if they do understand you.

In general, the human brain has difficulty processing sentences longer than 34 words. Try to keep yours as short as possible and keep it simple.

You should remember that writing is a muscle that can be improved with regular training. The good news is that if you focus on your readers and have a service mindset, you'll be leaps and bounds ahead of the competition. After all, the future belongs to those who can connect and communicate effectively.

Chapter 36

The Rationale of Publishing in an Academic Journal

> If a person fails to understand the importance of rationale, he or she makes a rational mistake.
> —Laura Cheng

It promotes the visibility of your research.

It can be beneficial for a researcher, as well as the institution hosting the journal, to get a research project published in an accredited journal. Publications serve as a means of disseminating the research to others in a given field, including the scientific and practical contributions it contains. The purpose of this is to raise the awareness of scientific researchers and practitioners who share similar interests in their field about new knowledge and to enable the advancement of this knowledge.

The process of getting published in a high-quality journal may be more challenging, but it manifests an expert level of research and demonstrates an ability to conduct an in-depth study of a topic. In addition, it also reflects the status of the institution which hosted the publication.

Journals have an advantage over other types of publications.

The peer-review process of an accredited journal ensures that every article is scientifically reliable and valid through the process of peer review. Scientists need to ensure that the research process, the claims, and the conceptualisations made by the researchers are based on scientific principles.

Quality control is ensured by peer review.

Through peer review, you are guaranteeing the quality of your work. A peer review refers to the process by which a board of expert reviewers evaluates the articles submitted by researchers to ensure that the articles are relevant, of high quality, and adhere to the scientific standards and the editorial standards of the journal before deciding whether they should be accepted for publication. To remove bias from peer review, it is done blind, e.g., without the reviewer knowing the identity of the author. It is usually the editor of the journal that organises the peer-review process.

How are journals ranked according to their impact factor?

To determine the status or relative importance of a journal in its field, there are several different ranking systems that are used. There are many ways to measure journal impact; the most well-known being the journal impact factor (JIF) developed by Eugene Garfield, who established the Institute for Scientific Information, which is now owned and controlled by Thomson Reuters. Journal impact factor affects the average article in a journal by illustrating how frequently it is cited over a certain period in other articles in that journal.

Consequently, the ranking of a journal can serve as a metric to highlight the journal's quality as well as the value of a researcher, typically an academic professor, a PhD student, or a research fellow at an academic institution like USB.

Appointment and Promotion of Academics

In academic institutions, when it comes to recruitment, performance assessments, promotions, research fellowships, and awards, the number of articles that a researcher has published in a reputable journal in a particular year is considered when making decisions on the researcher's career. USB acknowledges that the quality of the articles published in journals can play a role in the appointment and promotion of academics.

Today there is also the use of alternative metrics (altmetric) to measure the impact of scholarly research. You can define altmetric as the number of downloads or statistics sourced from social media websites.

As a rule of thumb, it is best for a researcher's reputation to have an article published in a journal that has a higher JIF score.

Accredited Journals versus Non-Accredited Journals

It is important to note that in South Africa, an accredited journal is a journal subsidised by the Department of Higher Education and Training. A journal that is sponsored must meet strict quality criteria, including peer review, to receive funding.

It is only in South Africa that a distinction is made between accredited and non-accredited journals; accredited journals include thousands of international journals. The government, the Department of Higher Education and Training, only subsidises academic and research institutions if their research has been published in a reputable journal. Most other countries award funding after a funding application is accepted.

It is, therefore, ideal to publish your research in an accredited journal, as this will lead to the recognition of your research and to obtaining additional research funding as well. On the website of the Division for Research Development at Stellenbosch University, you can find a list of the subsidised journals.

How to Publish in a Journal after Research

Writing up a research report is the first step. As recommended by the editors of scholarly journals, it is good practise to send the article to a colleague for a sense-making review and, thereafter, for language editing before submitting it. There are specific guidelines for each journal, which must be strictly adhered to when submitting a manuscript.

If the article is accepted for review, the editor of the journal will forward it to a group of peer reviewers who will conduct a blind review. Normally, the peer reviewers will each advise the editor to either recommend approval of the article, which doesn't often happen on the first review; have it sent back for revision; or reject it. The process of revising an article continues until a final decision can be made about whether the article should be published.

> Rational errors are made if a person fails
> to understand the value of rationality.
> —Laura Cheng

Chapter 37

What Are the Benefits of Publishing Research Findings?

> Knowing the benefits is more important than knowing its features because benefits trump features.
> —Laura Cheng

> It is the results that matter to people, not the features.
> —Laura Cheng

When your research has already been conducted, and you have come up with conclusions that are based on facts, it is not only necessary, but is also a virtuous action for you to publish your work.

Rationale for Publishing

Advance the Body of Knowledge

Your discovery will certainly contribute to the body of literature on a particular subject by enriching it. It will strengthen the arguments of others while refuting those that they have raised in the past. Among other things, it will help shed light on issues that have not been resolved, and it will also help build theories.

It is important to keep in mind that a theory arises from a culmination of factors documented and discussed by many scientists. Based on the evidence that has been collected and analysed in a systematic manner, theories are plausible explanations for phenomena.

To put it simply, a theory is just a generalisation of what has been discovered up to this point. With the advent of new research tools, it is always possible that a new, better theory will be developed with the use of these new tools.

From a Novice to a Renowned Expert

It is likely that if you have conducted a lot of research on a particular topic or issue, you will gain credibility and become regarded as a leading expert in that field. If there will someday be a government or non-government organisation that will require consulting services in your research, you will certainly have an advantage over others who have not published anything yet.

Whenever you conduct your research, you will have to make sure that you do it correctly each time. Being able to do it correctly means that you have carried out a rigorous investigation.

To be considered rigorous, you must have applied a thorough, exhaustive, or highly-accurate review of literature, methodology, results, and conclusion(s) in your research. It is particularly important to focus on the methodology since, if it turns out to be flawed or if it cannot be replicated by others, the rest of the paper will also be deemed suspect or unreliable.

Government policy may be improved by your published paper.

Policymaking is heavily influenced by research findings. By making policymakers aware of your study's findings, good governance policies can be developed. It is known as science-based policymaking. Time, money, and effort can be saved by using this approach. Avoid costly mistakes.

Singapore's traffic congestion reduction policy was made more effective by conducting baseline research prior to the implementation of the policy. The results can then be compared before and after implementation.

There is a need for legislators to keep in mind the dynamics of the local setting in which order needs to be brought. In other words, simply copying laws from one place to another without considering the particular needs and concerns of the local population may not work.

There are many developed countries where researchers are viewed as key contributors to the formulation of policy by their governments. Although they aren't perfect, this could be one of the reasons for the progressive nature of those countries. Support for researchers usually comes in the form of grants or funds allocated to them specifically for research purposes.

Probably gain an advantage in your career if you publish your work.

You may be able to propel yourself towards success based on the number of quality publications that you have produced. There are several research institutions that recognise meritorious research work that advances knowledge and leads to innovations. You will also increase your chances of getting a promotion if you publish your work.

It is typical for large companies to spend a portion of their annual budget on research and development. Therefore, innovations are expected to generate higher incomes for large companies. This will be a great opportunity for you to gain some economic gain if you are tasked with developing such products.

Feeling of Satisfaction

The fact that you have been able to publish your research findings in a reputable scientific journal gives you inner confidence that you have been a good researcher. Having spent endless hours rewriting your manuscript and writing it again and again, you are finally rewarded for your efforts. Although it is a time-consuming process, the end justifies the means. The feelings we have cannot be bought. Be humble when you learn something new and don't let it get over your head for it always pays to be humble.

As a good practice, you may wish to present your findings in scientific gatherings relevant to your area of expertise before publishing your findings in a scientific journal. Involving colleagues in your research paper will help you improve it because of their critical comments as well as suggestions.

The benefits of publishing research findings are certainly not limited to the ones mentioned above. Despite all your suffering, the greatest benefit you will receive is to share your knowledge with the rest of the world to make it a better place for us all. Is your research of any use if you are the only one who is aware of it?

Chapter 38

An Introduction to Technical Writing

> Our words must be able to make a difference.
> —Laura Cheng

This chapter explains what technical writing is. It also shows you how to become a better technical writer, what factors determine whether you can develop a quality technical document, and why the field is changing so rapidly.

In the world of business and academics, technical writing is still a highly-sought-after skill. The need for technical writers is expected to increase by 10% since 2014. This is faster than the average growth rate for all occupations.

An Explanation of What Technical Writing Is

Documenting complex technical processes falls under technical writing today. These can be reports, executive summaries, or briefs. Technical writing is any written communication of technical information at work.

There is a wide variety of high-tech manufacturing, engineering, biotech, energy, aerospace, finance, IT, and global supply chain companies that can fit into this category.

No longer do we have to read lengthy user manuals. Technical information must be clear and concise. These can be technical reports, e-mails, policies, briefs, and press releases.

Technical writing is commonplace in technical fields.

What is a technical writer?

In terms of the nature of the work that a technical writer does, it will differ depending on the industry and company that they work for. A technical writer's most important task is to take the highly-complicated and sometimes-confusing subject matter and convert it into a digestible and easy-to-understand way.

It is important in a variety of industries, especially in biotech, engineering, manufacturing, software, and healthcare.

It is not uncommon for technical writers to work on multidisciplinary teams, acting as a liaison between more-technically-oriented employees and less-technically-oriented readers. During the process of developing a communication plan, they will be closely involved with their teams.

Writing is not their only responsibility. The entire project must be understood from high-level goals to implementation details.

Education Requirements

While the educational background of a technical writer may vary, many professionals in this field hold a BA in English with an emphasis in writing, journalism, communications, curriculum development, IT, software, or engineering. Many technical writers have a master's degree in technical writing as well.

It is imperative that, regardless of how they acquire technical writing expertise, either through formal education or through job experiences, a good technical writer will be able to translate technical terms into layman's terms. Good technical writing skills are as important as good communication skills.

Does business writing differ from technical writing?

It sounds a lot like business writing.

A business writer, on the other hand, focuses on business plans, case studies, e-books, and marketing materials. In other words, they have an excellent understanding of business management and strategy.

A technical writer, on the other hand, has a strong aptitude for science, engineering, or information technology. Instruction manuals, guides, technical product descriptions, and research reports are among the documents they compile.

Different Types of Technical Writing

- Documentation for end-users and assistance guides
- Articles in medical and scientific journals
- Documentation pertaining to technical aspects
- Reports on technical topics
- Communications related to technical marketing, such as e-mails
- Reports on technical corporate matters
- Study of the feasibility of the project
- Documents related to white papers
- Findings from the research

Defining the Project Requirements

- Aim for conciseness
- Maintain accuracy
- Thoroughness throughout the whole process
- Based on collaboration, clear communication among all participants
- Part of the teaching element of logic and order

Industry Needs in Major Industries

- Economy/finance sector
- Centred on health
- Technology, science, and engineering
- For governments
- Educational programs
- Manufacturing

The variety of technical documents may seem overwhelming at first. Every document draws on a common set of skills and uses a similar process. Developing a process can be applied to any technical document.

> Our words need to have the power to
> make a difference when we write.
> —Laura Cheng

Chapter 39

Researchers' Errors in Journal Compliance

Many manuscripts are submitted daily to journals. However, not all of them are accepted for publication. One of the most important achievements of a researcher's academic career involves getting their research published.

Researchers strive to publish their work in high-impact journals. Publishing research is not an easy undertaking, and manuscript rejection is a common occurrence in academic writing. Every researcher will encounter manuscript rejection at some point in their career.

> There are no failures in science, and researchers can learn from their mistakes to ensure a smooth publication journey for their next paper.
> —Laura Cheng

This chapter will provide an overview of the most common journal compliance errors that authors make, leading to their rejection.

Failure to Follow Journal Guidelines

In most cases, authors miss checking the journal guidelines when drafting a manuscript, resulting in non-compliance with the guidelines.

Inaccurate Titles

There is a serious writing error when an incorrect title does not indicate the scope and limits of a study. If an experiment is conducted in a laboratory to determine corrosion inhibition properties, it should be made clear that the test was performed under controlled conditions. Otherwise, the article may be misleading.

Inaccuracies in the Abstract

It is common for abstracts to be presented several months prior to the paper being published. The abstract of a paper should be updated with more recent data after the paper has been written. In other words, make sure that the results and conclusions in the abstract are the same as those in the original paper.

Incomplete Introduction

In an introduction, the study question, hypothesis, and objectives should be presented. It is considered a major writing deficit if the above information is not provided and the importance of the study is not clearly explained.

Inexplicable Methods

Rather than writing, authors report previously-published methods that are like those used in the present study. In other words, the author simply reuses the methods section from paper to paper. Copying such material exactly constitutes self-plagiarism.

In addition, the methods should be updated according to the current research project. If some of the results do not seem to be related to the methods described or cannot be obtained by these methods, it is disconcerting.

Omissions of Results

Occurrence of errors during the writing of the results is common. As a result of adhering to the word limit, some information is often omitted, intentionally, without justification, or unintentionally. As an example, not all study subjects are included, or the names of statistical tests are not provided for specific analyses.

Irrational Discussion

It is imperative that the discussion is organised logically. Here are some common errors to avoid when writing the discussion:

There is a disconnect among ideas, and the flow of information is not well supported.

Content wanders from the results.

The presentation is biased and omits key findings from other researchers who have been conducted in the field.

There is insufficient explanation of key results.

The study is overstated in terms of its importance or its implications.

The description of the limitations of the study is not given.

Data Inconsistencies

Manuscripts often contain data that is inconsistent. There are instances when the same data is repeated as well. In some cases, however, the figures given in the text don't match those in the tables or figures. In summary, all these discrepancies relating to the data cause the manuscript to fail to comply with the journal's requirements, and consequently, the manuscript will be rejected.

Grammar and Punctuation Errors

Grammar errors are among the most common errors that authors overlook. Manuscripts may also contain grammatical errors and inconsistencies in style. Editors may reject manuscripts for these reasons as well.

Multiple Submissions of the Same Article

Even though many authors are unaware of it, the duplicate publication is against publication ethics. The same manuscript, or even part of it, cannot be submitted simultaneously to two journals. As a result, journals often don't publish such manuscripts as they believe the novelty of the research will be lost.

Lack of Thorough Literature Review

To highlight the novelty of the research topic, one should review several related studies during the literature review. Failure to do so may result in a topic being repeated and consequently rejected.

Conflict of Interest with Participants in Clinical Research

Research participants' identities are usually kept confidential in cases of clinical research. In some cases, however, case reports may include photographs or text that may reveal the identity of the participant. The practice is unethical, and journals tend to reject such manuscripts if they identify them.

Long and Incorrect Conclusion

A conclusion section should be brief and related to the text and data discussed in the results and discussion sections of the paper. Journals may require revisions of manuscripts in cases where this is not the case.

Reference Inconsistencies

Typically, manuscripts contain missing references, incorrect references that differ from those cited in the text, and incorrectly-formatted references. Such errors compromise the credibility of a paper.

Incomplete Documentation

The journal submission process requires the submission of several other related documents in addition to a well-written manuscript. Among them are forms related to authorship, conflicts of interest, ethical board approval, etc. However, authors find this step cumbersome and frequently submit incorrectly-filled-out or incomplete forms. This, in turn, delays publication, in some cases even leading to rejection, by causing unnecessary back-and-forth between the editorial board and the authors.

The information provided in this chapter will inform researchers and help them avoid having their manuscripts rejected.

www.ingramcontent.com/pod-product-compliance
Lightning Source LLC
Chambersburg PA
CBHW030930180526
45163CB00002B/523